UNIT A

Life Cycles

Theme: Models

THINK LIKE A SCIENTIST

HITCHING A RIDE

Living things produce offspring that, as adults, look very much like themselves. In this photo a Chinese water dragon gives a ride to one of her offspring. The Chinese water dragon is a lizard that lives in southeastern Asia. These lizards can grow up to 61 cm (24 in.) in length. They often rest on tree limbs that overhang bodies of water, such as lakes and ponds. With her baby clinging to her, a mother lizard, such as the one shown, can dive into the water to escape if an enemy threatens.

THINK LIKE A SCIENTIST

Questioning In this unit you'll study how animals and plants grow, change, and produce young. You'll investigate questions such as these.

- What Is a Life Cycle?
- How Do Flowering Plants Make Seeds?

Observing, Testing, Hypothesizing In the Activity "Look at What You've Become," you'll make a model home for mealworms. Then you'll observe how the mealworms grow and change. You'll also hypothesize why some mealworms grow faster than others.

Researching In the Resource "Going Around in Cycles," you'll find out about the life cycles of two other insects—the butterfly and the grasshopper.

Drawing Conclusions After you've completed your investigations, you'll draw conclusions about what you've learned—and get new ideas.

LIFE CYCLES OF ANIMALS

Think about some animals that you know. What were they like when they were young? How did they change as they grew older? Do you think all members of the animal kingdom grow and change throughout their lives?

• •

PEOPLE USING SCIENCE

Biologist Would you like to be alone in a small plane with a large bear? Jay Hammond, a biologist and bush pilot, was flying high above the Alaskan wilderness. Suddenly his passenger, a 275-kg (600-lb) bear, started to awaken. The bear had been drugged to keep it calm during the flight.

Minutes later, Hammond landed and unloaded the bear on the shore of a lonely lake. Now wide awake, the animal ran off to find a new home. Here the bear will mate, raise cubs, and spend the rest of its life. Like all animals, it will grow and change.

How are animals alike in the ways they change? How are they different? To find out, read this chapter!

Coming Up

◄ Biologist Jay Hammond flew a bear to its new home.

WHAT IS A LIFE CYCLE?

Arrange these words in order—*teenager, child, adult, baby*. How did you do it? Each word names a stage in the life cycle of a human. All living things go through stages, or life cycles. In this investigation, you'll find out about the life cycles of some plants and animals.

Activity

The Changes Chart

How have you changed since you were a baby? How do other living things change during their life cycles? Find out.

Procedure

1. With your group, brainstorm a list of living things that you've observed near your home or school. **Record** your list in your *Science Notebook*.

2. Make a Changes Chart. Fold a strip of paper lengthwise into four equal sections.

 Math Hint *To fold a piece of paper into four equal sections, fold it in half. Then fold it in half again.*

3. Look at the list of living things you made in step 1. Choose one of the living things from your list.

4. In the left-hand section of the chart, **draw** a picture or **write** a description of how you think the plant or animal you chose looked when it was very young. For help, look at pictures in books. **Predict** how the plant or animal will change as it gets older.

5. In each of the other three sections of the chart, **draw** or **write** your ideas about how the animal will change. Do not name the animal.

6. Exchange Changes Charts with another group. Study the other group's chart. Name the plant or animal that this chart is about. Ask the other group if you guessed correctly.

Analyze and Conclude

1. **Make a plan** to test your predictions from steps 4 and 5.

2. Show your teacher your plan. Then carry it out. How do the predictions you recorded on your Changes Chart **compare** with what you found out?

INVESTIGATE FURTHER!

EXPERIMENT

Fold a paper strip into eight sections. In the sections write these ages: 1, 3, 5, 7, 9, 15, 25, 55. In the sections, write how you have changed. For the ages you have not reached, predict how you'll change.

Step 4

A7

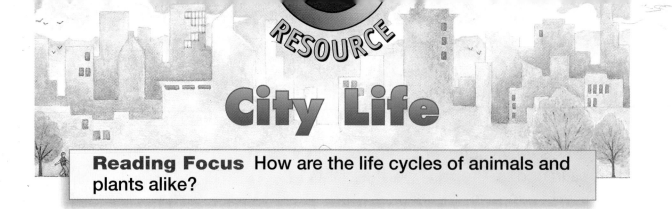

City Life

A city is full of life. People, ants, spiders, birds, squirrels, roses, and earthworms are only a few of the things that live in a city. You might have to look closely to see some forms of city life. But if you observe the living things in a city over time, you'll notice that they change.

A chart showing how an animal changes is made in the activity on pages A6 and A7. All living things go through certain changes. These changes include growth, development, reproduction, and death. Growth refers to changes in size—that is, plants and animals becoming larger. Development refers to changes in plants and animals as they mature, or become adults. Reproduction is the process by which plants and animals produce offspring, or young of their kind. Death marks the end of each plant's or animal's lifetime.

Animals go through ordered life stages, as you can see in the pictures of the dogs below. After several

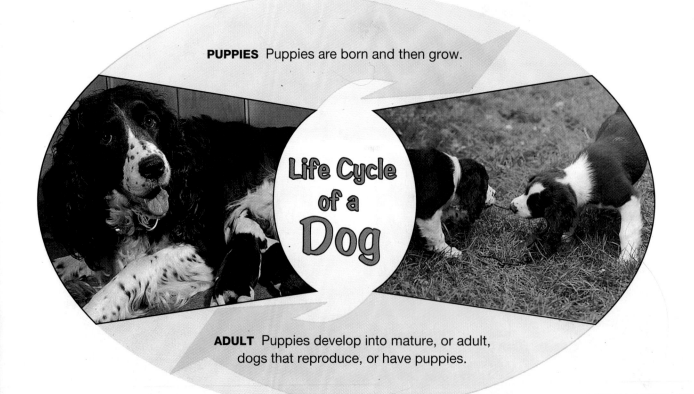

PUPPIES Puppies are born and then grow.

Life Cycle of a Dog

ADULT Puppies develop into mature, or adult, dogs that reproduce, or have puppies.

▲ **Living things in the spring**

years, an adult dog dies. But because it has reproduced, that kind of dog continues.

Plants go through life stages, too. A milkweed plant grows, blooms, and produces seeds. Some seeds fall to the ground. From these seeds new plants grow. The mature plant dies. But because it has reproduced, that kind of plant continues to exist.

Look at the two pictures above and below. What living things can you find? Compare the pictures. What changes have taken place in the living things over time?

The ordered stages that occur in a plant's or animal's lifetime are called a **life cycle**. A life cycle is like a circle. It has no end. One life cycle leads to another. ■

Living things in the summer ▼

What's Wrong With This Picture?

Reading Focus When ducks mate, why do they produce ducklings and not chicks?

If you heard that a duck had hatched out of a chicken egg, you probably wouldn't believe it. Animals produce young just like themselves. Chickens mate and produce chicks. Ducks mate and produce ducklings.

Chicks belong to one species (spē'shēz) and ducks belong to another species. A **species** is a group of living things that can produce living things of the same kind. Now do you know what's wrong with this picture?

Passed On or Learned?

Animals of the same species pass on certain traits to their offspring. A trait is a characteristic. It describes something. The offspring receive, or inherit, traits from their parents.

You and your classmates belong to the human species. Though each of you is special, you all have many of the same human traits.

Some things are not passed from parents to offspring. These things are learned. For example, having feet is a human trait that is passed from parents to children. But using your feet to kick a soccer ball is a skill you learn. Chicks hatch knowing how to peck for food. But suppose a chick pecks at a caterpillar that tastes bitter. The chick then learns to avoid that kind of food.

How Long Do Animals Live?

By producing young, each species can continue beyond the life span of each parent. An animal's life span is the time between its birth, or hatching, and its death.

Look at the table below. As you can see, each species' life span is different from another's. A spider's life span is only one to twenty years. Yet box turtles have been known to live as long as 123 years. About how long does an elephant live? ■

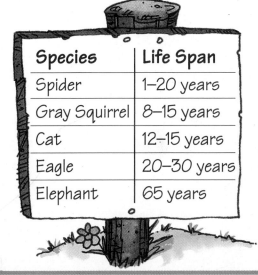

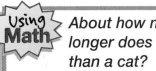

Using Math

About how many years longer does an elephant live than a cat?

Species	Life Span
Spider	1–20 years
Gray Squirrel	8–15 years
Cat	12–15 years
Eagle	20–30 years
Elephant	65 years

INVESTIGATION 1 WRAP-UP

REVIEW

1. What is a species?

2. What is a life cycle?

CRITICAL THINKING

3. What must happen so that the life cycle of a species does not end?

4. Explain the differences between inherited traits and those that are learned. Give two examples of each.

WHAT IS THE FIRST STAGE IN AN ANIMAL'S LIFE CYCLE?

A newborn kitten and a newborn puppy look *so* tiny. But each developed from something much tinier. What is that something? Find out and become an "eggs-pert" as you explore the first stage in an animal's life cycle.

Activity

Be "Eggs-act"!

To a scientist, observing something means much more than just looking. In this activity you must be "eggs-act" as you explore the first stage in a chicken's life cycle.

Procedure

1. Think of an uncooked egg cracked into a dish. **Make a drawing** in your *Science Notebook* to show the inside parts of the egg that you remember. If you can, label each part. Mark the drawing *A*.

2. Get an uncooked egg from your teacher. With your group, use a hand lens to **observe** the outside of the egg. **Draw** what you see.

 See **SCIENCE** and **MATH** **TOOLBOX** page H2 if you need to review **Using a Hand Lens.**

3. Crack the egg into a dish. Use the hand lens to **observe** the egg and the inside of the shell. **Draw** all the parts that you see. Mark this drawing *B*.

4. **Compare** drawing *A* with drawing *B*. What new parts did you discover?

Step 3

Analyze and Conclude

1. Based on the drawings your class did, do you think that all chicken eggs have the same parts? A chicken is a kind of bird. Do you think that all bird eggs have the same parts? How could you find out?

2. Each part you observed has a different job. Find the white spot on the yellow part of the egg. This spot could have developed into a new chick. **Infer** how the eggshell helps the developing chick.

INVESTIGATE FURTHER!

EXPERIMENT

Make a plan to study the eggs of another animal—for example, a fish. How are these eggs different from chicken eggs? How are they the same?

"Eggs-traordinary" Eggs!

Reading Focus How do the parts of an egg help an embryo grow?

Do you think eggs "eggs-ist" only to boil, poach, scramble, or fry? Actually, the job of an egg is to help produce offspring, or young. An **egg** is the first stage in the life cycle of almost all animals.

Some animals, such as baby horses, develop from eggs inside their mothers' bodies. Other animals, such as chickens, develop from eggs outside their mothers' bodies.

Eggs are "eggs-traordinary" in many ways. Even the tiniest egg contains everything needed for developing a new animal. Study the parts of the egg shown.

"Eggs-actly" How Would You Describe an Egg?

Eggs come in many shapes, colors, textures, and sizes. Chicken eggs, observed in the activity on pages A12 and A13, are round on one end and pointed on the other. Owl eggs are round. Plover eggs are

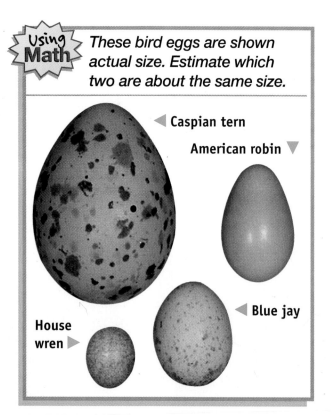

Using Math *These bird eggs are shown actual size. Estimate which two are about the same size.*

◀ Caspian tern

American robin ▼

Blue jay ◀

House wren ▶

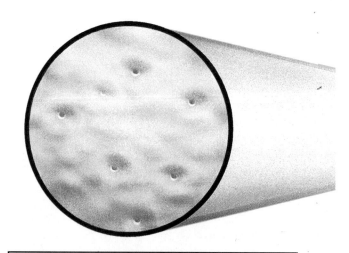

PORES A close-up look at tiny openings, called pores, in the shell of a chicken egg. Pores let water and oxygen enter the egg and carbon dioxide leave.

pear-shaped. Tortoise eggs are shaped like globes and sand grouse eggs like tubes.

Eggs can be brightly colored, dull, plain, or very fancy. From green and blue to black and red, eggs can be freckled, speckled, spotted, or dotted.

There are many kinds of egg coverings, too. Bird eggs have hard, chalky shells. Fish and frog eggs have a soft outer covering. They don't dry out, because they're laid in water. Slug and snail eggs have shiny, round shells.

Inside a Bird Egg

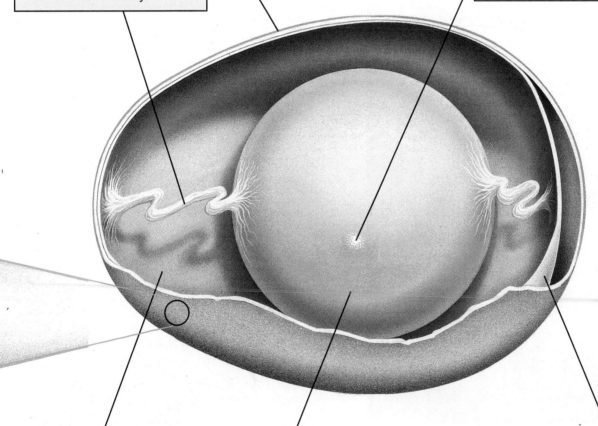

TWISTED STRANDS Twisted strands of the shell lining keep the embryo upright as the mother turns her egg. Turning the eggs warms them evenly.

SHELL The egg is covered by a shell. The shell protects everything inside the egg. A material called calcium makes the shell hard and helps to form the embryo's bones.

EMBRYO The white spot is where the embryo begins to grow. The **embryo** (em′brē-ō) is the developing chick. By the twenty-first day, the chick will start to hatch.

EGG WHITE The egg white cushions the embryo and provides it with water.

YOLK The yolk is the stored food for the embryo.

SHELL LININGS Just inside the shell are the shell linings. At the rounded end of the egg is an air space, which allows the embryo to get oxygen.

A15

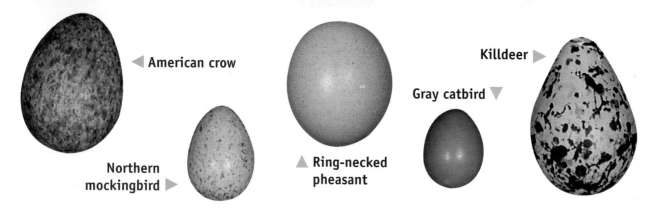

American crow ◀

Killdeer ▶

Gray catbird ▼

Northern mockingbird ▶

▲ Ring-necked pheasant

Ostrich eggs are the largest in the world. Each ostrich egg is about 16 cm (6 in.) long and has a mass of about $1\frac{1}{2}$ kg (3 lb). Compare the size of the ostrich egg with the size of the hummingbird egg in the picture below.

▲ A tiny hummingbird egg compared with an ostrich egg

"Eggs-actly" How Many?

The number of eggs that an animal lays varies with the species. The hornbill lays only 1 egg a year, but an oyster lays 500 million eggs a year. Chickens lay almost 1 egg a day, or up to 350 eggs a year. Each time an ocean sunfish produces eggs, it makes about 300 million.

Not every egg produces young. The eggs you eat do not contain embryos. For a chick or another animal to begin growing inside an egg, the mother must first mate with the father. Then—just think—the egg can grow into all the parts of an animal's body. An egg really is "eggs-traordinary"! ■

INVESTIGATE FURTHER!

EXPERIMENT

You can't easily see pores in a shell, but you can prove they are there. Place an egg in a clear container. A brown egg is best to use. Cover the egg with water. Don't touch or move the egg for 20 minutes. Use a hand lens to observe the shell. How has the shell changed? What do you think caused the change?

Hatching Chicks

Reading Focus What is an incubator and what is its function?

An incubator (in′kyo͞o-bāt ər) is a device that provides enough warmth, water, and fresh air to help keep something alive. An incubator in a hospital may help a tiny baby grow stronger. Other incubators are found on large chicken farms. These incubators are used to hatch eggs. Incubators for eggs, like the one shown here, come in two parts—the setter and the hatcher. Read the captions to find out the difference. ■

The trays in the setter move to turn the eggs many times each day. Eggs are warmed to a temperature of 37°C (99°F).

Large fans keep the air moving around the eggs.

1 SETTER Chicken eggs are placed on trays and loaded into a setter. Some setters are as large as rooms and can hold thousands of eggs at one time. The eggs stay in the setter for 18 days.

2 HATCHER On the nineteenth day, the eggs are put into metal or plastic baskets and moved to the hatcher. After 2 or 3 days in the hatcher, baby chicks hatch out of the eggs.

The Baby Book

Reading Focus What are two animals that are born live and two animals that hatch?

Almost all animals come from eggs. Some animal babies develop from eggs inside their mothers' bodies. Those babies are born live. Other offspring develop from eggs outside their mothers' bodies. Those babies hatch. Whether born live or hatched, each baby develops from a single egg.

Here are some baby animals from around the world. Look at the pictures and read about them. Which were born live? Which were hatched?

Baby African elephants grow inside their mothers' bodies for nearly two years. When a baby elephant, called a calf, is finally born, it weighs as much as a fully grown man. ▼

WALLABY

▲ Wallabies, from Australia, belong to the kangaroo family. A baby wallaby is called a joey. It is born live. Then it wriggles into its mother's pouch, where it drinks its mother's milk until it is about eight months old.

This mother crocodile from Egypt carries her hatched babies into the water to protect them from enemies. She will crack the eggs that are slow to hatch inside her mouth and let the babies wiggle into the water. ▼

ELEPHANT

CROCODILE

BEAR

◀ This bear cub had a mass of less than $\frac{1}{2}$ kg (1 lb) when it was born live. The rings of fur around its eyes make it look as if it's wearing spectacles, or eyeglasses. The spectacled bear is the only kind of bear that lives in South America.

OWL

PENGUIN

▲ These baby snowy owls hatched in a nest on the ground. Their home in the far north is a cold place called the tundra (tun′drə). Both parents care for their chicks. All the chicks are born with white fluff, which later turns gray. The gray color helps to hide the young owls from enemies.

▲ Gentoo penguins live in the Antarctic. The penguin parents take turns sitting on the nest. Both parents feed and care for the chicks that hatch. When the young penguins are about nine weeks old, they swim out to sea and live on their own.

=== INVESTIGATION 2 WRAP-UP ===

THINK IT WRITE IT

REVIEW

1. What is the first life-cycle stage in animals that hatch and in animals that are born live?

2. Draw and label the parts of a bird egg that help an embryo grow.

CRITICAL THINKING

3. On page A15 you read about the parts of an egg. Explain what would happen to the developing chick if each part didn't work.

4. What may happen to a chick embryo if the shell has a small crack in it? Explain.

HOW DO SOME ANIMALS GROW AND CHANGE?

Have you ever worn a costume and found that no one knew you? As some animals go through their life cycles, they change so much that you may not know what animals they are. Find out about one animal as it grows and changes.

Activity

Look at What You've Become

Imagine how you will change as you grow up. Do all animals change in the same ways you do? The animals in this activity are masters at some amazing changes. Find out what they are.

MATERIALS
- goggles
- plastic gloves
- 5 mealworms
- dry cereal without a sugar coating
- thin slices of apple and potato
- dish with a cover
- hand lens
- metric ruler
- *Science Notebook*

SAFETY
Wear goggles and gloves when handling the mealworms. Wash your hands when you have finished.

Procedure

1. Look at the list of materials with your group. **Predict** what a mealworm needs in order to survive. Explain which material meets which need. **Infer** which material might provide a mealworm with water.

2. Use the materials to make a home for the mealworms. In your *Science Notebook*, **describe** the home you made. Place the mealworms in the home.

3. Every two days, clean the home and give the mealworms fresh food.

Step 4

4. **Observe** the mealworms with a hand lens each day for three weeks. Use a ruler to **measure** changes in size. **Make a chart** to **record** any changes you observe.

5. **Make a bar graph** of your data. **Compare** your graph with the graphs of other students in your class. Continue to **observe** your mealworms as they become adults.

See **SCIENCE** and **MATH TOOLBOX** page H3 if you need to review *Making a Bar Graph.*

Analyze and Conclude

1. How did the mealworms change?

2. The adult stage of this insect is called a beetle. How many different stages did you observe in the life cycle of the mealworm beetle? **Draw** each stage.

3. **Hypothesize** why some mealworms grew faster than others.

Technology Link **CD-ROM**

INVESTIGATE FURTHER!

Use the **Best of the Net—Science CD-ROM**, Life Sciences, *Sockeye Salmon*, to find out about the unusual life cycle of a sockeye salmon. And find out the names of three other types of Pacific salmon.

Going Around in Cycles

▲ People grow and change. How has this person changed?

Your life cycle is special. You are first a baby, then a child, then a teenager, and then an adult. Suppose you saw a baby picture of an adult. You'd probably be able to say who the baby in the picture grew up to be. But if you saw an insect such as a butterfly in an early stage, you might not know what the animal was.

A Four-Stage Cycle

There are four stages in the life cycles of most species of insects, including butterflies, moths, flies, and beetles. The stages in order are (1) egg, (2) larva, (3) pupa, and (4) adult. Each stage looks very different from the stage before it and the stage after it.

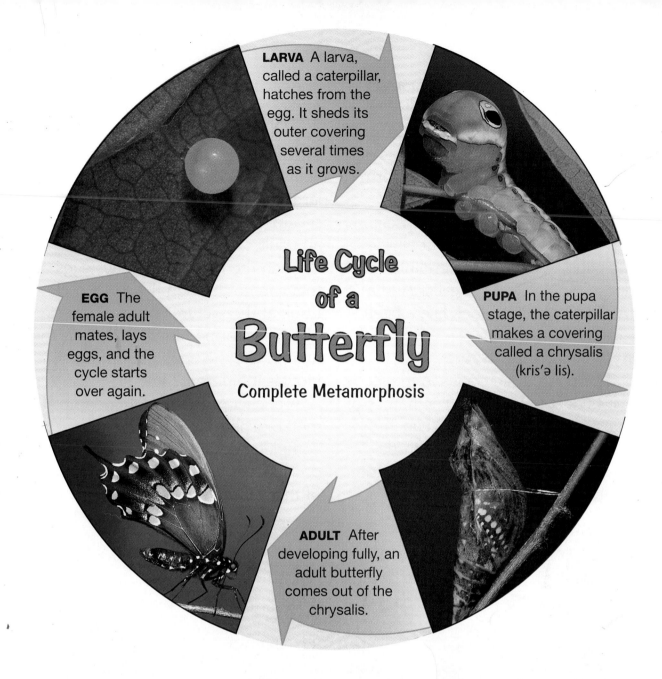

Life Cycle of a Butterfly

Complete Metamorphosis

LARVA A larva, called a caterpillar, hatches from the egg. It sheds its outer covering several times as it grows.

PUPA In the pupa stage, the caterpillar makes a covering called a chrysalis (kris′ə lis).

ADULT After developing fully, an adult butterfly comes out of the chrysalis.

EGG The female adult mates, lays eggs, and the cycle starts over again.

A four-stage life cycle is called **complete metamorphosis** (met ə-môr′fə sis). The first stage is the egg. The second stage, called the **larva** (lär′və), is a wormlike stage that doesn't look at all like the adult. The larval stage of certain insects has a special name. Look at the pictures. What is the butterfly larva called?

The larva eats and grows and then makes a covering for itself. At that time, the insect is in the third stage,

called the **pupa** (py$\overline{oo}$′pə). Inside the pupa, the adult insect develops. When it is fully developed, the adult insect comes out. The **adult** is the last stage of a life cycle. The adult female insect then mates and lays eggs, and the pattern continues.

Internet Field Trip

Visit **www.eduplace.com** to find out more about the life cycles of butterflies.

The beetle also goes through complete metamorphosis in its life cycle. The activity on pages A20 and A21 used mealworms, the larvas of beetles. The larva of the mealworm beetle is called a grub.

Now you can see that an insect in some stages doesn't look at all like the adult. A caterpillar certainly doesn't look like a butterfly. And a mealworm doesn't look like a beetle.

A Three-Stage Cycle

There are three stages in the life cycles of some insects. The names of the stages in order are (1) egg, (2) nymph, and (3) adult. A three-stage life cycle is called **incomplete metamorphosis**.

As with all animals, the first stage in the life cycle is the egg. The animal in the second stage, called a **nymph**, looks almost like a small adult. As the nymph eats and grows larger, it sheds its outer covering several times and then develops into an adult.

Then the female adult lays eggs that can go through the same cycle. Look at the pictures of the life cycle of a grasshopper. In what ways is the nymph like the adult grasshopper? How is it different?

A cricket goes through incomplete metamorphosis. A fly goes through complete metamorphosis. What life-cycle stages would take place in each of these insects?

Science in Literature

**Insect Metamorphosis
From Egg to Adult**
by Ron and Nancy Goor
Atheneum, 1990

INSECT INVASION

"In 1987, an enormous brood of millions of cicadas hatched out. If you took a walk late at night, you would see hundreds of cicadas crawling across streets. They covered every upright surface—even blades of grass. Their mating song was deafening. Such a gigantic brood of cicadas will appear again in 2004."

A cicada is a flying insect that takes 17 years to undergo metamorphosis! You can read more about this insect's invasion in the book *Insect Metamorphosis: From Egg to Adult* by Ron and Nancy Goor.

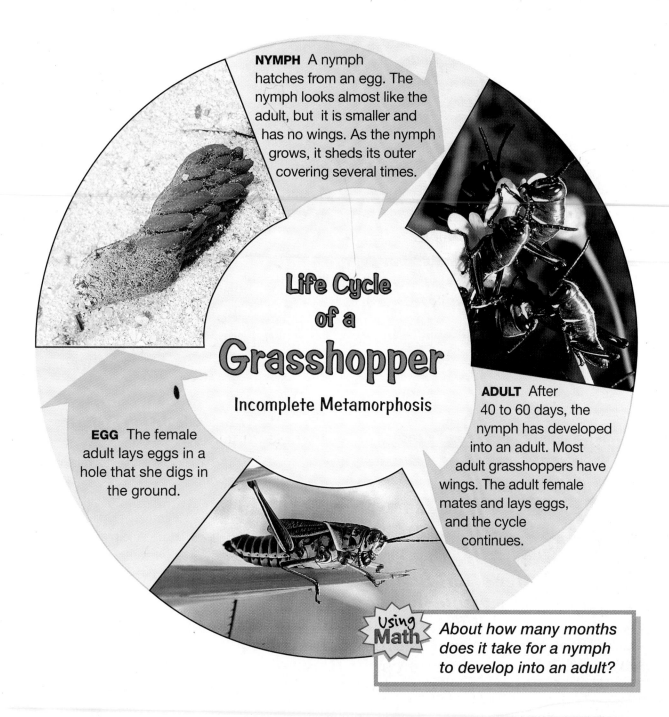

Life Cycle of a Grasshopper

Incomplete Metamorphosis

NYMPH A nymph hatches from an egg. The nymph looks almost like the adult, but it is smaller and has no wings. As the nymph grows, it sheds its outer covering several times.

ADULT After 40 to 60 days, the nymph has developed into an adult. Most adult grasshoppers have wings. The adult female mates and lays eggs, and the cycle continues.

EGG The female adult lays eggs in a hole that she digs in the ground.

Using Math *About how many months does it take for a nymph to develop into an adult?*

INVESTIGATION 3 WRAP-UP

THINK IT WRITE IT

REVIEW

1. What are the four stages in the life cycles of most species of insects?

2. What life-cycle stage is a caterpillar?

CRITICAL THINKING

3. A scientist identifies a wormlike animal as the larva of an insect. What do you think are the stages in the life cycle of this insect?

4. How are complete and incomplete metamorphoses the same? different?

A25

INVESTIGATION 4

HOW DO ADULT ANIMALS CARE FOR THEIR YOUNG?

Have you ever had a sitter? Hiring a sitter is one way adult humans might care for their children. In this investigation you'll learn how animals differ in the ways they care for their young.

Activity

The Animal-Sitter's Guide

What's a sitter's job? Suppose an animal such as a baby whale or a young giraffe had a human sitter. What do you think that sitter would need to know to care for the young animals? In this activity you'll find out.

MATERIALS
- animal-sitting assignment cards in a box
- construction paper
- colored markers
- discarded magazines
- reference books
- *Science Notebook*

Procedure

1. Take a card from your group's animal-sitting assignment box. Look at the name of the animal on the card and **record** the name in your *Science Notebook*. Find out about the baby animal's needs and how the parents care for the baby. **Record** what you find out. **Infer** the care the baby animal should receive.

Step 1

panther

hawk

turtle

2. On a sheet of construction paper, write a list of instructions for an Animal-Sitter's Guide for the class. Give information that would answer questions such as these: What kind of food does the baby animal need? When does it sleep? Does it make unusual noises? What might threaten or harm the baby animal?

Step 2

3. Include a drawing or picture of your animal.

4. Put your instructions in the class Animal-Sitter's Guide, where others can refer to them.

Analyze and Conclude

1. What would be the hardest part of taking care of the animal you wrote about? Explain your answer.

2. Compare the care needed by your animal with the care needed by other baby animals in the Guide. Which animal would be the hardest to sit for? Which would be the easiest? Explain your answers.

UNIT PROJECT LINK

For this Unit Project you will make an Animal-Sitter's Guide and a Plant-Sitter's Guide. Predict which pets are hardest to care for. With your group, interview owners of different kinds of pets. Record the information in a special pet section of your Animal-Sitter's Guide.

Technology Link

For more help with your Unit Project, go to **www.eduplace.com**.

Out of Sight, Out of Mind

Reading Focus What are some adaptations that help sea turtles survive?

It's easy to forget about something that you can't see. "Out of sight, out of mind" is a short way to say this. This saying describes how some animals behave toward their eggs. For example, a cowbird lays her eggs, one at a time, in the nests of other, smaller birds. Then she flies away, never to see her eggs again. The "foster parent" birds care for their own offspring as well as for the young cowbirds. You can see that for the mother cowbird, her eggs are "out of sight, out of mind."

Survival Kit

How do animals that hatch from out-of-sight, out-of-mind eggs survive? One thing that helps cowbirds survive is that the adult females lay their eggs in the nests of smaller birds. Because the young cowbirds are larger than the other young birds, they get more food.

The behavior of the female cowbird is an adaptation. An **adaptation** (ad əp tā′shən) is a behavior or part of a living thing that helps the living thing survive.

2 The female lays her eggs.

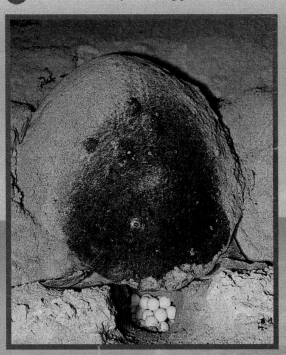

1 A female sea turtle swims to shore.

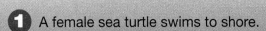

Many Eggs—Few Survive

Frogs and most fish lay many eggs but don't protect them. Laying many eggs is another animal adaptation.

A frog lays thousands of jelly-covered eggs. Many frog eggs become food for other animals. The frog eggs that do survive develop into tadpoles. Some tadpoles become food for snakes. Although a frog lays thousands of eggs, few eggs survive to develop into adult frogs. Laying many eggs, then, is an adaptation that helps frogs survive as a species.

Some animals hide their eggs before leaving them. Hiding eggs is also an adaptation. It is a way that animals help their offspring survive.

A female sea turtle crawls out of the sea at night. Using her flippers as shovels, she digs a nest in the sand. She lays at least a hundred eggs in the nest. The sea turtle's flippers, used as shovels, are also adaptations. They are a part of a living thing that helps it to survive.

After the sea turtle lays the eggs in the nest, she covers them with sand. Then she crawls back into the sea and never sees her young.

Although the female sea turtle has laid many eggs, probably only one baby turtle out of a hundred will survive. Other animals, such as raccoons, steal eggs from turtle nests. When the surviving eggs do hatch, the baby turtles crawl toward the sea. But sea birds swoop down upon them for food. And many of those that reach the water become food for sea animals. You can see how laying many eggs is an adaptation that helps sea turtles survive as a species. ■

3 The baby turtles hatch.

4 The baby turtles crawl to the sea.

A Whale of a Baby

Reading Focus What are some ways that a female whale cares for her young?

Did you know that the world's biggest baby is about 8 m (26 ft) long and has a mass of about 1,800 kg (2 T)? It's longer than a station wagon and weighs as much as a small truck. This baby is a blue whale calf. The blue whale calf's mother is much bigger than her baby. She's about 30 m (100 ft) long and has a mass of over 90,000 kg (100 T). That's as long as two big tractor-trailers and heavier than the largest dinosaur. A land animal's legs couldn't support that mass. But ocean water can.

A Whale of a Birth

A whale develops inside a mother whale and then is born live. Whales are born underwater in early winter, almost a year after the mother and father mate. A mother whale is called a cow. The baby is a calf. Normally, the calf slithers out of the cow, tail first.

The mother watches the newborn calf float to the surface. There the calf takes its first deep breath and sends up a fountain of mist from the blowhole on top of its head.

A mother humpback whale with her calf ▼

From the time it is born, the calf can swim. For several weeks the calf swims close to its mother. She gently strokes the calf with her flipper. A mother whale never leaves her baby unattended. She watches as it takes in fresh air before diving and as it blows out its warm breath when surfacing.

To feed, the calf dives underwater, where its mother squirts rich, warm milk into its mouth. A blue whale calf drinks about 500 L (132 gal) of milk every day and gains about 90 kg (200 lb) a day.

▲ **A closeup look at baleen**

A Whale of a Journey

One kind of whale is called a humpback. During the winter, the mother whales never eat. They live off their stored fat. But in the spring, thousands of humpbacks head for the colder waters of the Arctic, where there is food. For protection the whales swim in small groups called pods. On this long journey north, the mother whale watches out for dangers. Killer whales can hurt and even kill a baby humpback whale. A whale can get caught in nets dragged by fishing boats. Then it can't swim to the surface to breathe. A mother whale will protect her baby even if it means that she is putting herself in danger.

A Whale of a Summer

By summer, humpback whales arrive at the Arctic. The waters there are their feeding grounds. Since the mother whale hasn't eaten for six months, she's hungry. She will eat a year's worth of food—probably a ton a day—in the next six months.

Humpback whales don't have teeth. Instead, they have baleen, or flat bony plates that hang down from the roof of the mouth like the teeth of a comb.

Humpback whales feeding (*left and below*).

Using Math

A baby humpback whale is about 1,800 kg at birth. If it doubles its weight in one year, about how much does a one-year-old calf weigh?

The mother whale gulps big mouthfuls of sea water. She closes her mouth part way and then squirts the water out. She swallows the food that is trapped by the baleen. A whale's mouth can hold a ton of food.

All summer, as the mother whale eats and her calf drinks milk, they build up layers of fat. They play together. They slap the water with their tails. They roll over. Sometimes the little whale breaches—it hurls itself out of the water, twists high in the air, and lands with a splash!

A Whale of a Whale

In the fall the whales travel south toward warmer waters. There the calf's mother may mate again.

The young humpback whale has grown strong. It can find its own food. Now only a year old, it has doubled its birth size. It is truly a whale of a whale. ■

INVESTIGATION 4 WRAP-UP

REVIEW

1. What are adaptations? Give an example.

2. Choose an animal that you learned about in this investigation. Describe the care that the animal gets as it grows and develops.

CRITICAL THINKING

3. Explain why laying many eggs is an adaptation for the survival of a species.

4. Compare the needs of a baby whale with those of a human baby.

REFLECT & EVALUATE

Word Power

Write the letter of the term that best matches the definition. *Not all terms will be used.*

1. First stage in the life cycle of almost all animals
2. Developing chick
3. Ordered stages in a plant's or animal's lifetime
4. Last stage of complete and incomplete metamorphosis
5. Behaviors that help a living thing survive
6. Group of living things that can produce living things of the same kind

a. adaptations
b. adult
c. egg
d. embryo
e. larva
f. life cycle
g. pupa
h. species

Check What You Know

Write the term in each pair that best completes each sentence.

1. The wormlike second stage of complete metamorphosis is the (nymph, larva).
2. The pecking behavior of a chick is (learned, inherited).
3. A four-stage life cycle in insects is called (complete metamorphosis, incomplete metamorphosis).

Problem Solving

1. A female sea turtle may lay a hundred eggs at one time. A female elephant gives birth to only one baby elephant at a time. How does each mother differ in the way she cares for her offspring?

2. How might your life be different today if you skipped the development that occurs between the ages of two and four?

A mealworm is the larva stage of a beetle. Draw what you think the stages in the life cycle of the beetle would look like. Label each stage.

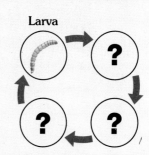
Larva

CHAPTER 2
LIFE CYCLES OF PLANTS

Many members of the plant kingdom grow from seeds. Have you ever planted a seed and watched it grow into a plant? What happened to the plant as time passed?

Connecting to Science
ARTS

Nature Poem Gwendolyn Brooks, an African American poet, tells in this poem about a child who plants a seed.

Tommy

I put a seed into the ground
And said, "I'll watch it grow."
I watered it and cared for it
As well as I could know.
One day I walked in my back yard
And oh, what did I see!
My seed had popped itself right out
Without consulting me.

—Gwendolyn Brooks

In this chapter you'll learn how plants grow and change. And you'll discover other things plants do "without consulting you."

Coming Up

◀ Planting flowers

WHAT IS THE FIRST STAGE IN THE LIFE CYCLE OF A FLOWERING PLANT?

What a survival story! In Egypt, seeds buried for over 1,000 years were able to start a new life cycle. You'll dig up more about seeds in Investigation 1.

Activity

The Inside Story

Seeds come in many sizes. But even the smallest seed can begin a new plant life cycle. Find out what's inside a seed.

- - - - - - - - - - - - - - - -

Procedure

1. Use a toothpick to pry open the halves of one lima bean seed that was soaked overnight. With your group, **observe** the parts of the seed. Place the two halves so that their inside surfaces are facing up. **Draw** the two halves in your *Science Notebook*. **Draw** arrows that point to each part. Number the arrows.

MATERIALS

- goggles
- plastic gloves
- soaked lima bean seeds
- toothpicks
- water
- paper towels
- 2 sealable plastic bags
- stapler
- metric ruler
- tape
- hand lens
- *Science Notebook*

SAFETY //////

Wear goggles during this activity. Clean up any spills immediately.

Step 1

2. Place a piece of wet paper towel in a plastic bag. Staple the bag about 2 cm from the bottom. Pry open a second bean seed and separate the two halves. Place all four seed halves in the bag.

Step 3

 See **SCIENCE** and **MATH TOOLBOX** *page H6 if you need to review* **Using a Tape Measure or Ruler.**

3. Prepare a second plastic bag like the first one. Add four whole bean seeds to the bag. Seal both bags and tape them to a wall or bulletin board. **Record** the date.

4. Use a hand lens to **observe** the whole seeds and seed halves each day. Add water as needed to keep the seeds moist. **Record** any changes. After three days, remove one of the whole seeds from its bag. Separate the halves. **Record** what you see. Every three days, remove another whole seed and separate its halves. **Record** all observations.

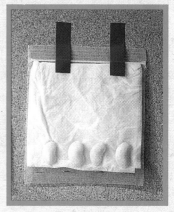

Analyze and Conclude

1. What changes occurred in the whole seeds? What changes occurred in the seed halves? **Hypothesize** about what might account for the differences.

2. How many different seed parts did you find? **Describe** each part. Beside each description, write the number that matches the number of the same part on your drawing.

3. Based on your observations, **infer** which seed part provides food for the young plant that grows from the seed. Explain your inference.

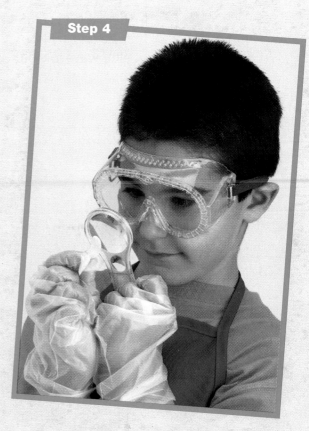

Step 4

It's "A-maize-ing"

Reading Focus When was maize first planted in Mexico?

Corn is one of the most important foods in the world. People and many kinds of farm animals eat corn. Corn, also called maize, can be used to make food products, such as cooking oil and bread. The time line shows how important corn has been.

Because the action in World War I has destroyed much of the farmland in Europe, the United States sends ships loaded with food to Europe. Corn and wheat from America save thousands of people from starving.

1920

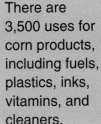
BEYOND 2000

Farmers grow different kinds of maize and invent better ways to store crops for winter.

800

1999
There are 3,500 uses for corn products, including fuels, plastics, inks, vitamins, and cleaners.

Maize is planted and harvested in Mexico. Seeds are gathered from wild plants.

2700 B.C.

1620
The Pilgrims land at what is now Plymouth, Massachusetts. Native Americans show the Pilgrims how to plant, grow, and use corn. The Pilgrims have a day of thanks, which we celebrate today as Thanksgiving.

A.D. 200
Maize, along with beans and squash, becomes a main part of people's diets in the Americas. Ways are found to increase the food production.

Plant Tricks

Reading Focus What are some ways that plants scatter their seeds?

Seeds can do stupendous tricks! Have you ever blown on the fluffy round head of a dandelion? Each little parachute that floats away is a seed that can produce a plant.

The Many Kinds of Seeds

The first stage in the life cycle of a flowering plant is a seed. Seeds are as different as the plants that grow from them. Seeds come in many sizes. A carrot seed is tiny. A coconut is a large seed. Seeds come in many shapes—round, pointed, oval, flat, and thin. They come in many patterns and colors—solid, speckled, white, brown, black, yellow, and red.

Whatever its size, shape, or color, a seed has three parts—a seed coat, stored food, and an embryo. Find out about these parts as you study the drawings below.

Seed Adaptations

Seeds are survivors. Plants have grown from lotus seeds that are centuries old. And seeds perform all kinds of tricks. Seeds can burst open, pop out, explode, fly, float, hitchhike, and parachute. These tricks help a seed get away from its parent plant. The new plant that develops from the seed may then get the things it needs to grow.

PARTS OF A SEED

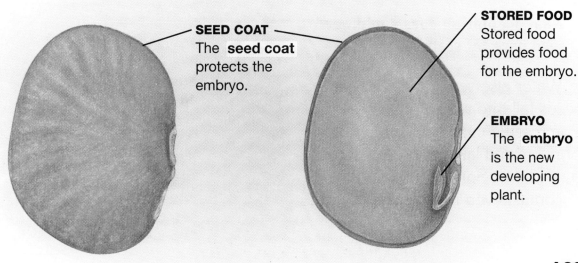

SEED COAT
The **seed coat** protects the embryo.

STORED FOOD
Stored food provides food for the embryo.

EMBRYO
The **embryo** is the new developing plant.

Wind scatters some seeds. As the tumbleweed plant is blown along the ground, its seeds scatter. Wind also blows seeds away from the parent plant. Some seeds have a shape that helps them travel in the wind. Because of its shape, the milkweed seed travels easily in the wind.

Animals also scatter seeds. As animals roam, their fur can pick up and carry sticky seeds. Animals, such as mice, carry seeds away and bury them. Birds carry seeds on their feathers and in their beaks. People sometimes carry seeds on their clothing.

▲ **Seed in a bird's beak**

What Seeds Need

A seed needs warmth, air, and moisture to **germinate** (jʉr′mə-nāt), or sprout. In the activity on pages A36 and A37, a wet paper towel in the bags provided moisture for the seeds. When a seed is in the ground, a tiny hole in the seed coat allows moisture to enter the seed. In addition to warmth and water, a seed needs oxygen from the air before it can germinate.

▲ **What adaptation does a milkweed seed have for scattering?**

Water also scatters seeds. Lotus seeds fall into water and float away. Some settle in the muddy bottoms of rivers and lakes and grow into new plants. Some seeds, such as coconuts, even float across oceans.

▼ **Sticktight seeds in a squirrel's fur**

With the proper conditions, a seedling develops. A **seedling** is a new plant that develops from an embryo. The growing plant has adaptations that help it get what it needs to grow. Some plants have long taproots that can reach far underground for water. Other plants have fuzzy stems and leaves that capture and hold in moisture.

▼ **A bean seedling**

Seed Plants Not From Seeds

All seed plants produce and can grow from seeds. However, some can also grow from trailing plant stems called runners or from underground plant parts called tubers (tōō′bərz). A strawberry plant produces runners. A potato is an example of a tuber. Plants, such as tulips, can grow from bulbs. Some plants can even grow from a piece of stem or leaf. But all seed plants produce seeds.

Runners, tubers, bulbs, and cuttings don't produce seedlings— only seeds produce seedlings. Seedlings develop into plants that produce food. This food is used by the plants and by animals that eat the plants. ■

Internet Field Trip
Visit **www.eduplace.com** to see amazing images of how seeds travel through air, in the sea, and on animals.

INVESTIGATION 1 WRAP-UP

THINK IT
WRITE IT

REVIEW

1. What is the first stage in the life cycle of a flowering plant?

2. List three adaptations of seeds that help scatter them.

CRITICAL THINKING

3. In Chapter 1 you found out about the stages in the life cycles of animals. How is the seed stage in the life cycle of a flowering plant like the egg stage in an animal's life cycle?

4. Suppose you planted seeds but they did not grow. Explain what seeds need to germinate. Tell what may have gone wrong with the seeds you planted.

HOW DO FLOWERING PLANTS MAKE SEEDS?

Have you ever picked or chosen a flower for a friend? What helped you decide which one to take? Was it the scent, the color, or the interesting shapes of its parts? In this investigation you'll find out how each of these is important for flowers to make seeds.

Activity

It's a Flower! It's a Factory!

Have you ever heard about a factory that blooms? A flowering plant is a factory. What does this factory make? In this activity you'll find out about one of its products.

Procedure

1. **Examine** a flower carefully. **Make a drawing** of it in your *Science Notebook*. **Draw** an arrow to each part of the flower. Label any part that you know.

2. Carefully pull the petals apart so that you can see the center of the flower. **Make a drawing** of what you see. Write questions about what you **observe**.

Step 2

A42

3. With your group, **compare** the parts of your flower with the photo shown. Label the parts on both of your drawings. What questions do you have about the parts of a flower?

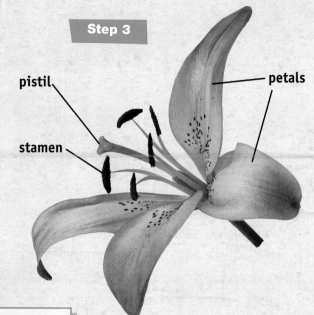

Step 3

pistil

petals

stamen

4. Gently shake your flower over a sheet of plain white paper. The small powdery objects that fall from the flower are grains of **pollen** (päl′ən). Use a hand lens to **observe** the grains. **Describe** how they look. **Record** your observations.

See **SCIENCE** and **MATH TOOLBOX** page H2 if you need to review **Using a Hand Lens.**

Analyze and Conclude

1. The **pistil** (pis′til) is the part of the flower where seeds form. Why do you think its location in the center is important?

Step 4

2. The **stamen** (stā′mən) is the part of the flower that contains pollen. For seeds to form in most plants, pollen must travel from a stamen of one plant to the pistil of another. Use a cotton swab to move pollen from a stamen to the pistil. **Hypothesize** how insects and birds might move pollen. **Talk with your group.** Explain your ideas and **record** your hypothesis.

3. A flower's petals attract insects, which feed on a sweet liquid in the plant. What is it about petals that might attract insects?

The Fantastic Flower

Reading Focus How does a flower produce a seed?

Many seed plants produce flowers. Flowers grow in many colors and sizes. Many people enjoy the beauty and smell of flowers so much that they give flowers as gifts on special occasions.

Plant Parenthood

Flowers might be called the parents of plants. A flower is part of an adult flowering plant. Seeds are formed in flowers. It is through the seed that the life cycle of the parent plant can continue.

Each flower has three parts that help a flower carry out its parent role. Their names are pistil, stamen, and petals. Look at the picture as you read about each part.

PARTS OF A FLOWER

PISTIL The **pistil** is the part of a flower where seeds develop and grow.

PETALS **Petals** are the brightly colored parts of a flower. Petals attract the insects and birds that pollinate flowers.

STAMEN The **stamen** produces **pollen**, a powdery material that is needed to make seeds form. Pollen must land on a pistil to make seeds form. This process is called **pollination** (päl ə nā′shən).

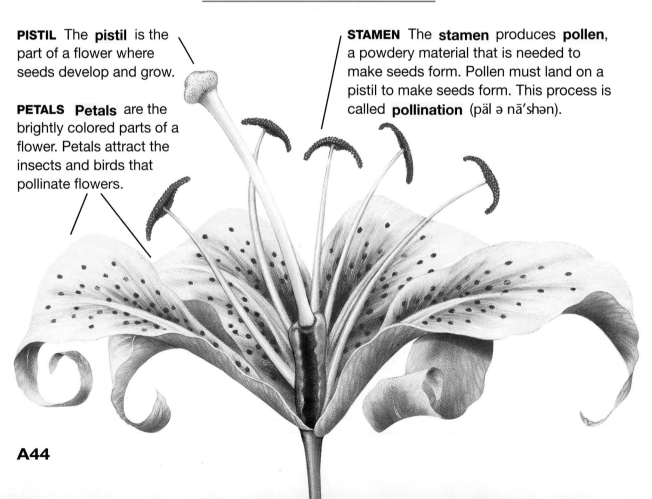

Seed Protection

Do you like to eat fruit? Did you know fruits come from flowers? A **fruit** is the part of a flower that forms around a seed. Pea pods, tomatoes, and apples are all fruits that we eat. A fruit protects the seed or seeds inside of it.

A fruit also provides a way for the seeds to be scattered. For example, birds like to eat cherries. Inside each cherry is a single seed, which is protected by a hard shell. When a bird swallows a cherry, it digests the soft part of the fruit. But the seed passes unchanged through and out of the bird's body. If the seed falls on the ground, it can grow into a new cherry tree.

Birds also like to eat blackberries, but they do not like blackberry seeds.

▲ Fruits protect seeds.

The birds push the seeds aside and wipe them off their beaks. The tiny seeds fall to the ground, where they can grow into new blackberry bushes.

Plant Helpers

Insects help in the pollination of flowering plants. For example, bees are attracted to the bright colors of a flower's petals and to a sweet-tasting nectar (nek′tər) inside the flower.

Pollen grains, observed in the activity on pages A42 and A43, have a sticky coating. When an insect comes to feed on the nectar in a flower, pollen grains cling to the insect's body. They then carry the pollen to the pistil of the same flower or to the pistil of another flower.

▼ **A tomato is a fruit.**

Not all flowers are pollinated by insects. Sometimes pollen is carried by wind and water. Birds and other animals, attracted by a flower's color and scent, can also carry pollen from one flower to another.

The hummingbird hovers over a flower and pushes its long beak deep into the flower to get the nectar. Pollen from the flower sticks to the bird, which then carries the pollen to the next flower.

Bats help pollinate flowering trees. Bats drink the nectar and eat the pollen. They transfer the pollen stuck on their tongues and noses from flower to flower.

▼ **Parent plant**

Flower Child

Plants produce seeds that develop into new offspring. The offspring will inherit many of the same traits as the parent plants. For example, the seeds of a tall pea plant will likely grow into another tall pea plant. Flower color and seed color are examples of other traits that are passed from parents to offspring. Look at the parent plant and its offspring shown below. What traits did the offspring inherit from its parent?

Plant Cycles

The life cycles of flowering plants vary greatly in length. The life cycles of some trees, for example, may be hundreds or even thousands of years long! Many of the flowering plants you know have yearly life cycles. Such plants are called annuals because they live for only one year or one season. Study the life cycle of a flowering plant shown on the next page.

▼ **Offspring plant**

LIFE CYCLE OF A FLOWERING PLANT

POLLINATION
The flowers open and are ready to be pollinated.

SEED FORMATION
After pollination, the flower withers. Seeds develop and are scattered.

GROWTH
The plant grows and flower buds appear.

SEEDS
In spring the seeds absorb water and begin to swell.

GERMINATION
A seed germinates. A stem, leaves, and roots develop.

INVESTIGATION 2 WRAP-UP

REVIEW

1. Describe the three main parts of a flower. Tell how each part helps seeds form.

2. Explain the difference between pollination and germination.

CRITICAL THINKING

3. You are having lima beans and tomatoes at dinner tonight. What plant parts are you eating? How are they different? How are they alike?

4. Write a short story about what would happen if something stopped the pollination of flowers.

HOW DO PLANTS WITH CONES MAKE AND PROTECT SEEDS?

Have you ever seen pine cones used to decorate something? For a pine tree, cones are more than just decoration. In this investigation you'll find out just what cones do for a plant.

Activity

Cone Sweet Home

Think of some ways your home protects you. In this activity you'll find out how cones provide protection for seeds.

Procedure

1. A cone is a plant part that grows on a tree called a conifer (kän'ə fər). **Examine** some cones. **Record** questions you have about plants that make cones. **Record** your observations in your *Science Notebook*.

2. With your partner, **classify** the cones. Each group of cones should share at least one trait. Remember, a trait is a characteristic. Use traits such as size, color, and shape.

3. Look at the pictures of conifers on the next page. What kinds of conifers did your cones come from?

▲ **Cedar cone**

Pine cone ▲

Spruce cone ▶

4. A cone is made of woody parts called scales. Carefully pull off several scales from each cone. A conifer seed grows on the scale where the scale joins the cone. With a hand lens, **observe** the scales to find a seed. **Make a drawing** of what you observe on the scales.

Pine tree

Step 4

5. Look at the picture of the cone scale at the right. **Compare** the picture with your drawing.

Spruce tree

Analyze and Conclude

1. Some cones can open and close. Cones close in damp weather. How might this action help cones? Cones open and release seeds in dry weather. **Talk with your group** and **infer** what one job of a cone is.

2. How are the cone of a conifer and the fruit of a flowering plant alike?

Cedar tree

Evergreens

Reading Focus How do conifers reproduce?

Many trees shed their leaves in the fall as part of their life cycles. But other trees have leaves (or needles) all year long. Such trees are called evergreens because they're always green. Actually, evergreens do shed their leaves, but most grow new ones at the same time. That's why they're always green.

Pine, spruce, fir, hemlock, and cedar trees are all evergreens. These evergreen trees have something else in common—they all bear cones. But not all evergreens produce cones. Those that do are called conifers. The word *conifer* means "cone-bearing." A **cone** is the part of the conifer that produces pollen or seeds.

There are two kinds of conifer cones. Pollen cones make and release pollen, much as the stamen of a flower does. Seed cones receive

DIFFERENT KINDS OF EVERGREENS

Eastern hemlock ▶

Douglas fir ▶

fish scales   roof shingles   cone scales

the pollen and use it to make seeds. Each cone is a woody stalk covered with stiff **scales**, which protect the seeds under them. The activity on pages A48 and A49 shows that the scales overlap, like the scales on a fish or the shingles on a roof.

The Life Cycle of a Conifer

What happens to the seeds of cone-bearing evergreens? Some are eaten or carried away by animals.

Those seeds that are lucky enough to land on good, rich soil and receive enough warmth, moisture, and sunlight can grow into trees.

One good place for a seed to fall is on a rotting log. The log is rich in things that plants need to grow. So the log nurses the tiny seed as it sprouts and develops into a seedling. A log that feeds a seedling is called a nurse log.

As a seedling's roots grow down and its branches grow out, it develops into a young conifer. The young conifer grows taller and taller and produces cones. At the proper time, the seed cones open and their seeds fall to the ground. And the life cycle of the conifer continues.

◀ **White pine**

◀ **Blue spruce**

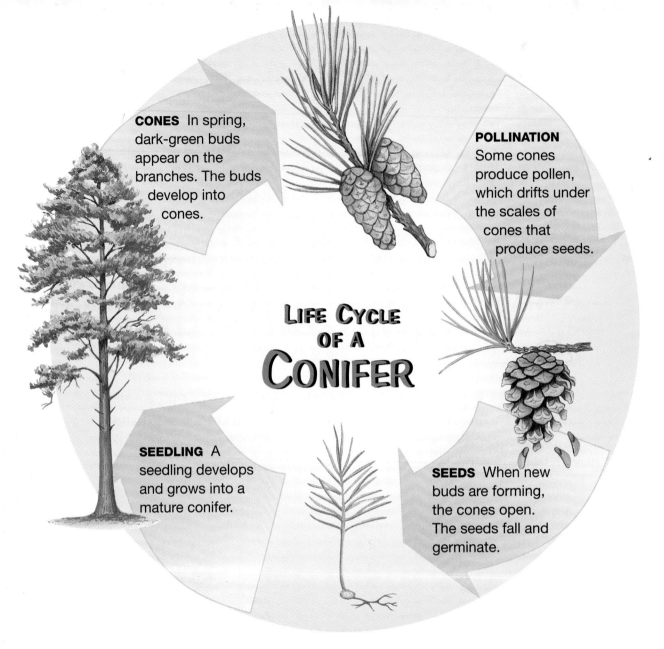

LIFE CYCLE OF A CONIFER

CONES In spring, dark-green buds appear on the branches. The buds develop into cones.

POLLINATION Some cones produce pollen, which drifts under the scales of cones that produce seeds.

SEEDS When new buds are forming, the cones open. The seeds fall and germinate.

SEEDLING A seedling develops and grows into a mature conifer.

Conifers, Water, and Fire

If you're like most people, you probably think that fire is always harmful to a tree's life cycle. You might also think that moisture is always helpful. Read on—you might be surprised at what you find out.

Everyone knows that plants need water. But sometimes, a conifer can get too much of a good thing. When the air is dry, the scales in the cones open, allowing air to enter. When there is a lot of moisture in the air, the scales close up tightly, because seeds need to be kept dry. Moisture can cause the seeds in a tightly closed cone to rot. So moisture is not always helpful.

Are forest fires always harmful? It's true that when fire hits the leafy top of a tree, the tree almost always dies. Shrubs and bushes also die. But the forest itself is not necessarily dead. In fact, some cones, such as those of the lodgepole and jack pines, actually *need* heat as hot as a

A52

A forest fire ▲   **Soon after the fire** ▲

fire just to open. These cones remain closed
until they reach a temperature as high as
about 50°C (122°F). The high temperature
melts the sticky pitch inside the cone, and the
cone opens. Then the seeds can be scattered.
Soon, some of the seeds germinate, and
seedlings appear. Fire may sometimes be
harmful to plants but not to cones that
contain the seeds for new conifers. ■

Within a year, regrowth begins. ▶

INVESTIGATION 3 WRAP-UP

THINK IT WRITE IT

REVIEW   **1.** Why are evergreens always green?

2. How do conifers make and protect seeds?

CRITICAL THINKING   **3.** What part of a cone do you think is most like the fruit of a flowering plant? Explain your answer.

4. Explain how a forest fire can be part of the life cycle of a conifer.

HOW DO PLANTS CHANGE DURING THEIR LIFE CYCLES?

You already know some changes that plants make during their life cycles. In this investigation you'll find out how some plants change as they grow and how they respond to changes around them.

Activity

Sizing Up Tree Growth

As you grow, the bones in your legs and arms get longer. What parts of a tree get longer when it grows? Find out.

Procedure

1. Look at the tree in the pictures. How did the tree change?

2. Compare the two trunks. **Record** your observations in your *Science Notebook*.

3. Compare the height of the lowest branch in each picture. **Compare** the length of the branches in each picture. **Record** your observations.

▲ **Young tree**

▲ **Full-grown tree**

4. A tree trunk grows about $2\frac{1}{2}$ cm bigger around each year. **Measure** the distance around the trunk of a tree at a height of about 120 cm off the ground. **Record** your measurement. **Estimate** the age of the tree.

Step 4

See **SCIENCE** and **MATH TOOLBOX** page H6 if you need to review **Using a Tape Measure or Ruler.**

5. Find out how branches grow. The place on a branch where growth is occurring is usually a different color from the rest of the branch. **Observe** some branches on two different kinds of trees. Look for color differences. Where do they occur? Remember to look at the branches, not the leaves. **Record** what you observe.

Analyze and Conclude

1. Based on your observations, **infer** where growth occurs on a branch. What happens to the branches of a tree as the tree ages?

2. How do the trunks of most trees change as the trees age?

INVESTIGATE FURTHER!

RESEARCH

How can you tell when a tree is sick or dying? Call a tree service and find out, or research diseases of trees in an encyclopedia or a book about plants. What changes caused by disease would you look for? What might cause the death of a tree? Share your findings with your class.

Activity

A Change of Plants

Do you squint when you walk into bright light? Find out how plants respond to changes in their environment.

MATERIALS
- goggles
- 3 seedlings, each growing in a paper cup
- shoebox with a lid that has a hole in it
- plastic wrap
- tape
- *Science Notebook*

SAFETY
Wear your goggles. Wash your hands after handling seedlings.

Procedure

1. Put one seedling into a shoebox. Make sure the soil is damp. Be sure the seedling is away from the hole in the lid and that it doesn't touch the top of the box. Put the lid on the box.

Step 1

2. Use a pencil to make a small hole in a sheet of plastic wrap. The stem of a seedling should just fit through the hole. Gently pull the seedling in the second cup through the hole. Tape the plastic wrap tightly to the cup, as shown.

3. Gently turn the cup upside down. Tape the cup to the bottom of a shelf or a desktop so that the seedling hangs upside down, as shown.

4. Place the third seedling on a flat surface where it can receive light.

5. **Talk with your group** and **predict** how each seedling will look in three days. **Record** your predictions in your *Science Notebook*.

6. After three days, **observe** the seedlings. **Record** any changes you observe. To check your results, **compare** them with those of your classmates.

Analyze and Conclude

1. **Compare** your observations with your predictions. What do you think caused any changes you observed?

2. If a plant does not adjust to changes, **infer** what might happen to it.

Step 2

Step 3

UNIT PROJECT LINK

Sometime you might be asked to plant-sit for a friend's plants. Ask people you know if they have had any problems in caring for their plants. Find out how the problems were solved. Record the problems and solutions in a Plant-Sitter's Guide.

Technology Link

For more help with your Unit Project, go to **www.eduplace.com**.

Where Are You Growing?

Reading Focus How do plants adapt to different conditions?

As children get older, they get bigger. As a plant goes through its life cycle, it gets bigger, too. The stem gets taller. The roots get longer. The roots and shoots grow more branches. All plants grow in these ways.

As shown in the activity on pages A54 and A55, plants also grow in another way. Their stems get bigger around. Imagine hugging a tree. You can reach around the trunk of a young tree. But you may not be able to do this after the tree has been growing for many years.

Responding to Light

If a bright light is shined in your eyes, you'll squint. Plants respond to light, too. Have you ever seen a photograph of a field of sunflowers? You may have noticed that all the flowers are turned the same way.

Plants respond to light by growing toward it. The seedlings grew toward the light in the activity on pages A56 and A57. If a plant is placed where it gets light on only one side, the stem of the plant will bend in the direction the light is coming from.

Amaryllis growing toward light ▶

Responding to Water

Plants take in water through their roots. Plant roots respond to water by growing in the direction where the water is found. For example, a willow tree is growing close to a riverbank. The tree roots that are nearer the river grow faster and in the direction of the river. The tree roots that are farther from the river are in drier soil. These roots grow very slowly.

A cactus has adaptations that help it survive in the dry desert. It has wide, shallow roots that allow it to take in rainwater quickly. A cactus also has a thick waxy stem and thin needle-like leaves. Both of these adaptations keep the plant from losing water.

Responding to a Pull

Roots and stems respond to the force of gravity, which pulls you toward Earth. Roots grow in the direction of the pull of gravity. So roots grow down. Stems grow in the direction opposite to the pull of gravity. So stems grow up. Even if you plant seeds upside down, the stems will grow up and the roots will grow down.

▲ **How is a cactus adapted to the desert?**

Science in Literature

FOREST FIRE!

"At last huge storm clouds darken the sky. Thunder grumbles through the forest. But before the rain begins to fall, a brilliant bolt of lightning slashes into a dead tree. Orange flames sweep down its trunk until they lick the dry forest floor. In an instant the flames are darting along the ground, burning up everything in their path."

To find out what happens next, read *A Tree in a Forest* by Jan Thornhill. You will learn how a 212-year-old maple tree grew and changed over its lifetime. Enjoy this amazing story about plants and animals who live together in the forest.

A Tree in a Forest
by Jan Thornhill
Simon & Schuster, 1991

Plant Protection

Besides responding to light, water, and gravity, plants also respond to living things in their environment. Many plants have special adaptations that help protect them from living things that can harm them.

Quills and thorns are adaptations. Think of porcupines. They protect

▲ **Sharp thorns of musk thistle**

▲ **Poison ivy leaves grow in threes.**

themselves with quills. Some plants protect themselves with thorns. Thorns seem to say, "Stay away!"

Some plants, such as poison ivy, produce chemicals that protect them. Poison ivy can cause an itchy rash on someone who handles the plant. Mature milkweed plants are harmful for cattle and sheep to eat.

Protecting the life cycle of a plant protects the species. Species that can't protect themselves may die out. ■

INVESTIGATION 4 WRAP-UP

THINK IT WRITE IT

REVIEW

1. Describe two ways that plants respond to gravity.

2. Give two examples of adaptations that help protect a plant.

CRITICAL THINKING

3. Scientists have put experiments on the space shuttle to see how plants grow in a weightless environment. How would roots and stems be affected? Predict some of the problems in growing seeds in space.

4. Explain one change in a plant's environment that can cause a growth change in the plant.

REFLECT & EVALUATE

Word Power

Write the letter of the term that best matches the definition. *Not all terms will be used.*

1. Part of the flower that produces pollen
2. New plant that develops from an embryo
3. Woody parts of a cone
4. Part of a flower that forms around a seed
5. Part of the flower where seeds develop and grow
6. Powdery substance formed in the stamen

a. fruit
b. germinate
c. pistil
d. pollen
e. scales
f. seed coat
g. seedling
h. stamen

Check What You Know

Write the term in each pair that best completes each sentence.

1. The new developing plant is the (fruit, embryo).
2. The stamen is the part of the flower that produces (seeds, pollen).
3. A fruit is likely to contain (seeds, pollen).
4. The word *conifer* means ("evergreen," "cone-bearing").

Problem Solving

1. In the park, you notice squirrels collecting acorns, children picking flowers, and a bird building its nest. Explain which activities might help plant pollination.

2. If the conifers in a forest did not produce cones one year, how would their life cycle be affected?

On a separate sheet of paper, make a larger copy of this drawing of a flower. Color the flower parts with these colors: pistil—orange, stamen—blue, and petals—red. Label the parts.

Finding the Main Idea

One goal in reading science is to find the important ideas and the facts that support those ideas. To find the main idea, follow clues such as the topic sentence, title, headings, or words in bold print. A topic sentence is often the first sentence of a paragraph.

Look for these clues to find the main idea.
- Topic sentence
- Title, headings
- Words in bold print

Read the paragraph below. Then complete the exercises that follow.

The Baby Book

Almost all animals come from eggs. Some animal babies develop from eggs inside their mothers' bodies. Those babies are born live. Other offspring develop from eggs outside their mothers' bodies. Those babies hatch. Whether born live or hatched, each baby develops from a single egg.

1. Write the letter of the sentence that states the main idea of the paragraph.

  a. Some animal babies develop from eggs inside their mothers' bodies.

  b. All eggs hatch outside the mother's body.

  c. Other offspring develop from eggs outside their mothers' bodies.

  d. Almost all animals come from eggs.

2. What is the important clue that helped you find the main idea?

Using Math **Analyze Data**

The average heights of some different types of trees are shown in this table.

Average Heights of Some Trees in the United States	
Type of Tree	Height (m)
Ash	30
Birch	25
Fir	75
Oak	50
Redwood	132
Walnut	20

Use the data in the table to complete these exercises.

1. What is the difference between the average height of the tallest tree and that of the shortest tree?

2. Which tree has an average height that is three times that of the birch tree?

3. When a fir tree is 10 years old, it is about 1 m tall. Compare your height with that of a 10-year-old fir.

4. How much greater is the average height of a redwood tree than that of an oak tree?

5. Which tree has an average height that is one half the average height of the oak tree?

6. The average height of which tree is 10 m less than the average height of an ash tree?

7. What is the average height of a redwood tree rounded to the nearest hundred? to the nearest ten?

8. Write the average heights of the trees in order from least to greatest.

9. Make a bar graph of the data in the table.

On your own, use scientific methods to investigate a question about life cycles, growth, or change.

THINK LIKE A SCIENTIST

Ask a Question

Pose a question about living things that you would like to investigate. For example, ask, "How does the color of light affect the growth of seedlings?"

Make a Hypothesis

Suggest a hypothesis that is a possible answer to the question. One hypothesis is that seedlings will grow faster under colored light than under white light.

Plan and Do a Test

Plan a controlled experiment to compare the effects of white light and blue light on seedling growth. You could start with seedlings, two lamps, and a blue filter. Develop a procedure that uses these materials to test the hypothesis. With permission, carry out your experiment. Follow the safety guidelines on pages S14–S15.

Record and Analyze

Observe carefully and record your data accurately. Make repeated observations.

Draw Conclusions

Look for evidence to support the hypothesis or to show that it is false. Draw conclusions about the hypothesis. Repeat the experiment to verify the results.

WRITING IN SCIENCE
Note Taking

As you read in science, taking notes can help you recall important ideas. Do research to find out more about the growth of seedlings. Follow these guidelines for note taking.

- Write statements in your own words.
- Use short phrases.
- State the most important facts and ideas.
- List supporting details.

SCIENCE and MATH TOOLBOX

Using a Hand Lens

A hand lens is a tool that magnifies objects, or makes objects appear larger. This makes it possible for you to see details of an object that would be hard to see without the hand lens.

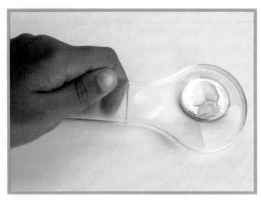

▲ Place the lens above the object.

▲ Move the lens slowly toward you.

If the object starts to look blurry, move the lens toward the object. ▶

Look at a Coin or a Stamp

1. Place an object such as a coin or a stamp on a table or other flat surface.

2. Hold the hand lens just above the object. As you look through the lens, slowly move the lens away from the object. Notice that the object appears to get larger.

3. Keep moving the lens until the object begins to look a little blurry. Then move the hand lens a little closer to the object until the object is once again in sharp focus.

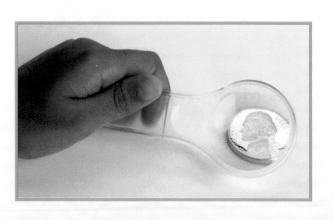

Making a Bar Graph

A bar graph helps you organize and compare data.

Make a Bar Graph of Animal Heights

Animals come in all different shapes and sizes. You can use the information in the table to make a bar graph of animal heights.

Heights of Animals	
Animal	**Height (cm)**
Bear	240
Elephant	315
Cow	150
Giraffe	570
Camel	210
Horse	165

1. Draw the side and the bottom of the graph. Label the side of the graph as shown. The numbers will show the height of the animals in centimeters.

3. Choose a title for your graph. Your title should describe the subject of the graph.

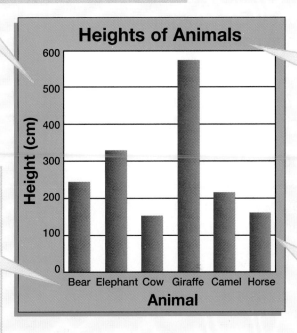

2. Label the bottom of the graph. Write the names of the animals at the bottom so that there is room to draw the bars.

4. Draw bars to show the height of each animal. Some heights are between two numbers.

Using a Calculator

After you've made measurements, a calculator can help you analyze your data.

Add and Multiply Decimals

Suppose you're an astronaut. You may take 8 pounds of Moon rocks back to Earth. The table shows the weights of the rocks. Can you take them all? Use a calculator to find out.

Weight of Moon Rocks	
Moon Rock	Weight of Rock on Moon (lb)
Rock 1	1.7
Rock 2	1.8
Rock 3	2.6
Rock 4	1.5

1. To add, press:

(1)(.)(7)(+)(1)(.)(8)(+)

(2)(.)(6)(+)(1)(.)(5)(=)

Display: 7.6

2. If you make a mistake, press the clear entry key (CE/C) once. Enter the number again. Then continue adding. (Note: If you press CE/C twice, it will clear all.)

3. Your total is 7.6 pounds. You can take the four Moon rocks back to Earth.

4. How much do the Moon rocks weigh on Earth? Objects weigh six times as much on Earth as they do on the Moon. You can use a calculator to multiply.

Press: (7)(.)(6)(×)(6)(=)

Display: 45.6

5. The rocks weigh 45.6 pounds on Earth.

clear entry

divide
multiply
plus
equal

Making a Tally Chart

A tally chart can help you keep track of items you are counting. Sometimes you need to count many different items. It may be hard to count all of the items of the same type as a group. That's when a tally chart can be helpful.

Make a Tally Chart of Birds Seen

These students are bird watchers. They're making a tally chart to record how many birds of each type they see.

Here are the tallies they have made so far.

Type of Bird	Tally
Cardinal	||
Blue jay	‖‖‖ ‖‖‖ ‖‖‖
Mockingbird	||||
Hummingbird	‖‖‖ ||
House sparrow	‖‖‖ ‖‖‖ ‖‖‖ ‖‖‖	
Robin	‖‖‖ ‖‖‖ ||

Every time you count one item, you make one tally.

When you reach five, draw the fifth tally as a line through the other four.

To find the total number of robins, count by fives and then ones.

You can use your tally chart to make a chart with numbers.

Type of Bird	Tally
Cardinal	2
Blue jay	15
Mockingbird	4
Hummingbird	7
House sparrow	21
Robin	12

What kind of bird was seen most often?

Now use a tally chart to record how many cars of different colors pass your school.

Using a
Tape Measure or Ruler

Tape measures and rulers are tools for measuring the length of objects and distances. Scientists most often use units such as meters, centimeters, and millimeters when making length measurements.

Use a Tape Measure

1. Measure the distance around a jar. Wrap the tape around the jar.

2. Find the line where the tape begins to wrap over itself.

3. Record the distance around the jar to the nearest centimeter.

Use a Metric Ruler

1. Measure the length of your shoe. Place the ruler or the meterstick on the floor. Line up the end of the ruler with the heel of your shoe.

2. Notice where the other end of your shoe lines up with the ruler.

3. Look at the scale on the ruler. Record the length of your shoe to the nearest centimeter and to the nearest millimeter.

Measuring Volume

A graduated cylinder, a measuring cup, and a beaker are used to measure volume. Volume is the amount of space something takes up. Most of the containers that scientists use to measure volume have a scale marked in milliliters (mL).

Measure the Volume of a Liquid

1. Measure the volume of juice. Pour some juice into a measuring container.

2. Move your head so that your eyes are level with the top of the juice. Read the scale line that is closest to the surface of the juice. If the surface of the juice is curved up on the sides, look at the lowest point of the curve.

3. Read the measurement on the scale. You can estimate the value between two lines on the scale.

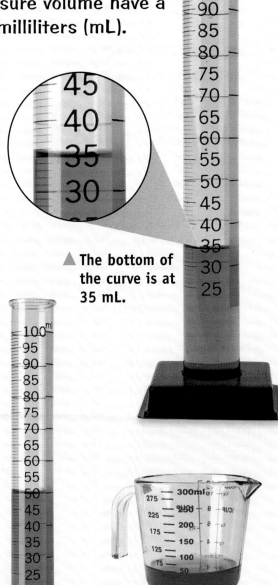

▲ The bottom of the curve is at 35 mL.

This beaker has marks for each 25 mL. ▶

This graduated cylinder has marks for every 1 mL. ▶

▲ **This measuring cup has marks for each 25 mL.**

Using a Thermometer

A thermometer is used to measure temperature. When the liquid in the tube of a thermometer gets warmer, it expands and moves farther up the tube. Different scales can be used to measure temperature, but scientists usually use the Celsius scale.

Measure the Temperature of a Cold Liquid

1. Take a chilled liquid out of the refrigerator. Half fill a cup with the liquid.

2. Hold the thermometer so that the bulb is in the center of the liquid. Be sure that there are no bright lights or direct sunlight shining on the bulb.

3. Wait a few minutes until you see the liquid in the tube of the thermometer stop moving. Read the scale line that is closest to the top of the liquid in the tube. The thermometer shown reads 21°C (about 70°F).

Using a
Balance

A balance is used to measure mass. Mass is the amount of matter in an object. To find the mass of an object, place it in the left pan of the balance. Place standard masses in the right pan.

Measure the Mass of a Ball

1. Check that the empty pans are balanced, or level with each other. When balanced, the pointer on the base should be at the middle mark. If it needs to be adjusted, move the slider on the back of the balance a little to the left or right.

2. Place a ball on the left pan. Then add standard masses, one at a time, to the right pan. When the pointer is at the middle mark again, each pan holds the same amount of matter and has the same mass.

3. Add the numbers marked on the masses in the pan. The total is the mass of the ball in grams.

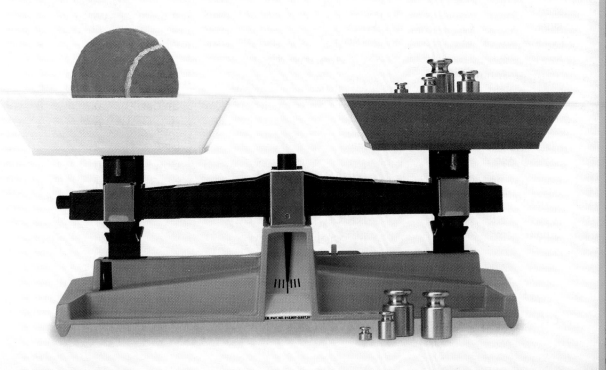

Making a Chart to Organize Data

A chart can help you keep track of information. When you organize information, or data, it is easier to read, compare, or classify it.

Classifying Animals

Suppose you are studying characteristics of different animals. You want to organize the data that you collect.

Look at the data below. To put this data in a chart, you could base the chart on the two characteristics listed—the number of wings and the number of legs.

My Data

Fleas have no wings. Fleas have six legs.

Snakes have no wings or legs.

A bee has four wings. It has six legs.

Spiders never have wings. They have eight legs.

A dog has no wings. It has four legs.

Birds have two wings and two legs.

A cow has no wings. It has four legs.

A butterfly has four wings. It has six legs.

Give the chart a title that describes the data in it.

Name categories, or groups, that describe the data you have collected.

Make sure the information is recorded correctly in each column.

Animals—Number of Wings and Legs

Animal	Number of Wings	Number of Legs
Flea	0	6
Snake	0	0
Bee	4	6
Spider	0	8
Dog	0	4
Bird	2	2
Cow	0	4
Butterfly	4	6

Next, you could make another chart to show animal classification based on number of legs only.

Reading a Circle Graph

A circle graph shows a whole divided into parts. You can use a circle graph to compare the parts to each other. You can also use it to compare the parts to the whole.

A Circle Graph of Fuel Use

This circle graph shows fuel use in the United States. The graph has 10 equal parts, or sections. Each section equals $\frac{1}{10}$ of the whole. One whole equals $\frac{10}{10}$.

Of all the fuel used in the United States, 4 out of 10 parts, or $\frac{4}{10}$, is oil.

Of all the fuel used in the United States, 3 out of 10 parts, or $\frac{3}{10}$, is natural gas.

Of all the fuel used in the United States, 2 out of 10 parts, or $\frac{2}{10}$, is coal.

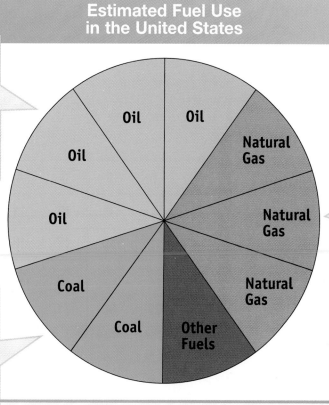

Estimated Fuel Use in the United States

Measuring
Elapsed Time

A calendar can help you find out how much time has passed, or elapsed, in days or weeks. A clock can help you see how much time has elapsed in hours and minutes. A clock with a second hand or a stopwatch can help you find out how many seconds have elapsed.

Using a Calendar to Find Elapsed Days

This is a calendar for the month of October. October has 31 days. Suppose it is October 22 and you begin an experiment. You need to check the experiment two days from the start date and one week from the start date. That means you would check it on Wednesday, October 24, and again on Monday, October 29. October 29 is 7 days after October 22.

Monday, Tuesday, Wednesday, Thursday, and Friday are weekdays. Saturday and Sunday are weekends.

Last month ended on Sunday, September 30.

October

Sunday	Monday	Tuesday	Wednesday	Thursday	Friday	Saturday
	1	2	3	4	5	6
7	8	9	10	11	12	13
14	15	16	17	18	19	20
21	22	23	24	25	26	27
28	29	30	31			

Next month begins on Thursday, November 1.

Using a Clock or a Stopwatch to Find Elapsed Time

You need to time an experiment for 20 minutes.

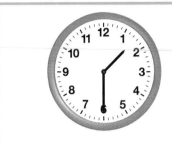

It is 1:30 P.M.

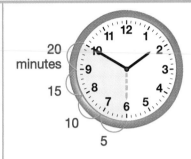

Stop at 1:50 P.M.

You need to time an experiment for 15 seconds.
You can use the second hand of a clock or watch.

60 seconds = 1 minute

Start the experiment when the second hand is on number 6.

Stop when 15 seconds have passed and the second hand is on the 9.

You can use a stopwatch.

Press the reset button on a stopwatch so that you see 0:00₀₀.

Press the start button. When you see 0:15₀₀, press the stop button.

MEASUREMENTS

Volume
1 L of sports drink is a little more than 1 qt.

Area
A basketball court covers about 4,700 ft². It covers about 435 m².

Mass and Weight
A basketball has a mass of about 650 g. It weighs about 1½ lb.

Metric Measures

Temperature
Ice melts at 0 degrees Celsius (°C)
Water freezes at 0°C
Water boils at 100°C

Length and Distance
1,000 meters (m) = 1 kilometer (km)
100 centimeters (cm) = 1 m
10 millimeters (mm) = 1 cm

Force
1 newton (N) =
   1 kilogram x meter/second/second
   (kg x m/s²)

Volume
1 cubic meter (m³) = 1 m x 1 m x 1 m
1 cubic centimeter (cm³) =
   1 cm x 1 cm x 1 cm
1 liter (L) = 1,000 milliliters (mL)
1 cm³ = 1 mL

Area
1 square kilometer (km²) = 1 km x 1 km
1 hectare = 10,000 m²

Mass
1,000 grams (g) = 1 kilogram (kg)
1,000 milligrams (mg) = 1 g

Temperature
The temperature at an indoor basketball game might be 25°C, which is 77°F.

Length/ Distance
A basketball rim is about 10 ft high, or a little more than 3 m from the floor.

Customary Measures

Temperature

Ice melts at 32 degrees Fahrenheit (°F)

Water freezes at 32°F

Water boils at 212°F

Length and Distance

12 inches (in.) = 1 foot (ft)

3 ft = 1 yard (yd)

5,280 ft = 1 mile (mi)

Weight

16 ounces (oz) = 1 pound (lb)

2,000 pounds = 1 ton (T)

Volume of Fluids

8 fluid ounces (fl oz) = 1 cup (c)

2 c = 1 pint (pt)

2 pt = 1 quart (qt)

4 qt = 1 gallon (gal)

Metric and Customary Rates

km/h = kilometers per hour

m/s = meters per second

mph = miles per hour

GLOSSARY

Pronunciation Key

Symbol	Key Words	Symbol	Key Words
a	cat	g	get
ā	ape	h	help
ä	cot, car	j	jump
		k	kiss, call
e	ten, berry	l	leg
ē	me	m	meat
		n	nose
i	fit, here	p	put
ī	ice, fire	r	red
		s	see
ō	go	t	top
ô	fall, for	v	vat
oi	oil	w	wish
͞oo	look, pull	y	yard
o͞o	tool, rule	z	zebra
ou	out, crowd		
		ch	chin, arch
u	up	ŋ	ring, drink
ʉ	fur, shirt	sh	she, push
		th	thin, truth
ə	**a** in **a**go	*th*	**th**en, fa**th**er
	e in ag**e**nt	zh	measure
	i in penc**i**l		
	o in at**o**m		A heavy stress mark (′) is placed after a syllable that gets a heavy, or primary, stress, as in **picture** (pik′chər).
	u in circ**u**s		
b	bed		
d	dog		
f	fall		

A

acid rain (as'id rān) Rain that contains a large amount of acids, and that results from the burning of fossil fuels. (D43) *Acid rain* can harm living things.

adaptation (ad əp tā'shən) Behavior or part of a living thing that helps it survive in a certain environment. (A28, E40) A rose's thorns and a camel's hump are *adaptations*.

adult (ə dult') The last stage of a life cycle. (A23) The butterfly is the *adult* stage of a caterpillar.

air pollution (er pə lōō'shən) Any harmful or unclean materials in the air. (D17) Burning fuels can cause *air pollution*.

aquifer (ak'wə fər) An underground layer of rock where ground water collects. (D31) The water in a well usually comes from an *aquifer*.

astronomer (ə strän'ə mər) A scientist who studies the origin, features, and motion of objects in space. (B14) *Astronomers* use telescopes, cameras, and space probes to study the stars.

atmosphere (at'məs fir) The layer of gases surrounding Earth or another planet. (B12, D8) Earth's *atmosphere* is made up of gases such as oxygen, nitrogen, and carbon dioxide.

atom (at'əm) The smallest particle of matter. (C20) Water is made up of the *atoms* of two different substances—hydrogen and oxygen.

axis (ak'sis) The imaginary line on which an object rotates. (B38) Earth's *axis* runs between the North Pole and the South Pole.

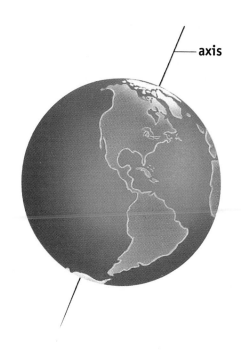

axis

B

behavior (bē hāv′yər) The way an animal typically acts in a certain situation. (E42) One *behavior* of pill bugs is to move toward moist, dark places.

C

camouflage (kam′ə fläzh) The ability to blend in with the surroundings. (E45) An animal's fur or skin can be *camouflage*, helping the animal hunt or avoid hunters.

carnivore (kär′nə vôr) An animal that eats only other animals. (E17) Wolves, cougars, lions, hawks, and owls are *carnivores*.

chemical change (kem′i kəl chānj) A change in matter in which different kinds of matter are formed. (C23) A *chemical change* occurs when wood burns and becomes gases and ash.

chemical property (kem′i kəl präp′ər tē) A description of how matter can change into another kind of matter. (C14) A *chemical property* of paper is its ability to burn.

community (kə myōō′nə tē) A group of plants and animals that live in a certain area and depend on one another. (E31) A pond's plants and animals form a *community*.

complete metamorphosis (kəm plēt′ met ə môr′fə sis) The four-stage life cycle of many insects. (A23) A life cycle that goes from egg to larva to pupa to adult is described as a *complete metamorphosis*.

compound machine (kam-pound mə shēn′) A machine that is made up of two or more simple machines. (C76) A pair of scissors is a *compound machine* because it contains two kinds of simple machines—a lever and a wedge.

condense (kən dens') To change form from a gas to a liquid. (C55, D29) When water vapor in the air cools, it *condenses* into tiny droplets of liquid water.

conduction (kən duk'shən) The movement of heat by direct contact between particles of matter. (C47) Heat moves by *conduction* from warmer matter with faster-moving particles to cooler matter with slower-moving particles.

conductor (kən duk'tər) A material that transfers heat or electricity easily. (C48) Metals are good *conductors* of heat.

cone (kōn) The part of a conifer that produces pollen or seeds. (A50) Each *cone* is a woody stalk covered with stiff scales.

constellation (kän stə lā'shən) A group of stars that form a pattern that looks like a person, animal, or object. (B46) Different *constellations* are visible from Earth at different times of year.

consumer (kən soom'ər) A living thing that eats other living things to survive. (E17) Animals are *consumers*.

controlled experiment (kən-trōld' ek sper'ə mənt) A test of a hypothesis in which the setups are identical in all ways except one. (S7) In the *controlled experiment*, one beaker of water contained salt; all the other beakers contained only water.

convection (kən vek'shən) The circulation of heat through a liquid or gas (fluid) by the movements of particles from one part of the matter to another. (C48) *Convection* takes place in a room with a heater: As hot air rises from the heater, cool air flows down to take its place.

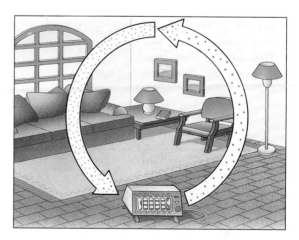

crater (krāt'ər) A bowl-shaped pit. (B11) *Craters* on the Moon and on Earth were formed by meteorites striking the surface.

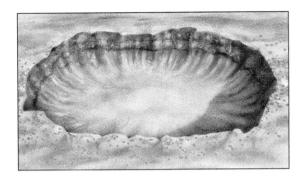

 D

decomposer (dē kəm pōz'ər) A living thing that breaks down and feeds on the remains of once-living things. (E18) *Decomposers* such as mushrooms recycle the remains of once-living things.

dormancy (dôr'mən sē) A decrease in plant activity during the winter. (E76) Sap flows in maple trees in the spring after the tree's *dormancy* during winter.

 E

earthquake (ɥrth'kwāk) A sudden movement of large sections of rock beneath Earth's surface. (D51) Books tumbled from shelves during the *earthquake*.

ecosystem (ek'ō sis təm) A place where living and nonliving things interact. (E64) The animals, plants, and insects in the tops of trees in a rain forest have their own *ecosystem*.

egg (eg) The first stage in the life cycle of almost all animals. (A14) Birds hatch from *eggs* outside the mother bird's body.

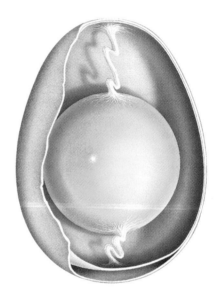

embryo (em'brē ō) An animal or plant in the earliest stages of its development. (A15, A39) A plant *embryo* is the tiny plant that is found inside a seed.

energy (en'ər jē) The ability to cause a change in matter. (C31) A car uses *energy* from gasoline or diesel fuel to run.

energy of motion (en'ər jē uv mō'shən) The energy that moving matter has. (C31) Sliding downhill on a sled, tossing a basketball into the air, and flying a kite in the wind are examples of *energy of motion*.

environment (en vī'rən mənt) All the surrounding living and nonliving things that affect a living thing. (E10) A drop of water, a rotting log, a desert, an ocean, and a rain forest are examples of different *environments*.

equator (ē kwāt'ər) An imaginary line that circles Earth halfway between the two poles. (B64) If you live near the *equator*, you live in a hot climate because your region receives direct sunlight most of the time.

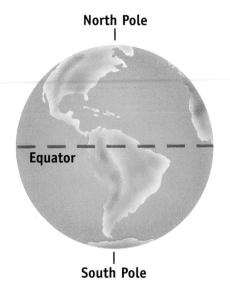

North Pole

Equator

South Pole

erosion (ē rō'zhən) The breaking up and moving of weathered rocks from one place to another. (D52) The Grand Canyon was formed by millions of years of *erosion*.

evaporate (ē vap'ə rāt) To change form from a liquid to a gas. (C54, D29) On a warm dry day, puddles on the sidewalk *evaporate* quickly.

extinction (ek stiŋk'shən) The permanent disappearance of all living things of a certain kind. (E20) The *extinction* of the saber-toothed cat is a mystery that some scientists are working to solve.

flare (fler) A bright area on the surface of the Sun caused by a solar storm. (B27) A solar *flare* is hotter than surrounding areas of the Sun and so is brighter.

food chain (fo͞od chān) The path that energy takes through a community as one living thing eats another. (E26) The first link in a *food chain* is usually a plant.

food web (fo͞od web) Two or more food chains that overlap and link. (E28) A *food web* connects animals through the plants and animals that they eat.

force (fôrs) A push or a pull. (C64) When you open a door, you apply a *force*.

fossil fuel (fäs′əl fyo͞o′əl) A fuel formed over time from the remains of plants or animals. (D10) *Fossil fuels* such as oil, coal, and natural gas are found underground.

freeze (frēz) To change form from a liquid to a solid. (C55) The loss of heat causes a liquid to *freeze*.

friction (frik′shən) A force that makes it hard for two objects to move past one another easily when the objects touch. (C46) *Friction* causes your hands to get warm when you rub them together.

fruit (fro͞ot) The part of a flower that forms around a seed. (A45) Cucumbers, tomatoes, oranges, peaches, and pears are *fruits*.

fulcrum (ful′krəm) The fixed point around which a lever turns. (C73) If you use a lever to lift an object, the *fulcrum* is located between you and the object you are lifting.

gas (gas) A state of matter that has no definite shape and does not take up a definite amount of space. (C20) A *gas* spreads out evenly to fill whatever space it is in.

germ (jʉrm) A tiny organism that can cause disease. (D37) Chlorine kills some of the *germs* in water.

germinate (jɥr′mə nāt) To sprout and begin to develop into a seedling. (A40) Most kinds of seeds need moisture, air, and warmth to *germinate*.

glacier (glā′shər) A large mass of slow-moving ice. (D53) When a *glacier* meets the sea, large chunks of ice fall off, forming icebergs.

gravity (grav′i tē) A force that pulls two or more objects toward each other. (B22, C65) To fly into space, a rocket must overcome Earth's *gravity*.

ground water (ground wôt′ər) The water found beneath Earth's surface. (D31) In some areas, *ground water* fills the small spaces that are between underground rocks, soil, and sand.

habitat (hab′i tat) The place where an animal or a plant lives. (E10) Deer live in a woodland *habitat*.

heat (hēt) The energy of moving particles of matter. (C32) Adding *heat* to matter causes its particles to move faster.

herbivore (hɥr′bə vôr) An animal that eats only plants. (E18) Cows and rabbits are *herbivores*.

hibernation (hī bər nā′shən) A deep sleep that helps some animals survive the winter. (E75) An animal that is in *hibernation* breathes slowly, has a slow heartbeat, and has a low body temperature.

hypothesis (hī päth′ə sis) An idea about or explanation of how or why something happens. (S6) The *hypothesis* that the Earth revolves around the Sun has been supported by evidence gathered by astronomers.

inclined plane (in klīnd′ plān) A simple machine with a slanted surface. It allows objects to be raised or lowered from one level to another without lifting them. (C74) A ramp is a kind of *inclined plane*.

incomplete metamorphosis
(in kəm plēt' met ə môr'fə sis)
The three-stage life cycle of some
insects. (A24) A life cycle that goes
from egg to nymph to adult is
called *incomplete metamorphosis.*

inexhaustible resource (in eg-
zôs'tə bəl rē'sôrs) A natural
resource that does not decrease, or
become used up, as people use it.
(D11) Wind can't be used up so it
is an *inexhaustible resource.*

insulator (in'sə lāt ər) A poor
conductor of heat or electricity.
(C48) Air that is trapped in the
small spaces between fibers of
clothing acts as an *insulator.*

larva (lär'və) The second stage
in the life cycle of an insect that
undergoes complete
metamorphosis. (A23) A butterfly
larva is called a caterpillar.

lava (lä'və) Liquid rock flowing
on the surface. (D51) Fires broke
out when *lava* reached the wooden
frames of houses.

lever (lev'ər) A simple machine
made up of a bar that turns, or
rotates, around a fixed point. (C73)
A *lever* helps to lift a heavy object
or a tight lid with less effort.

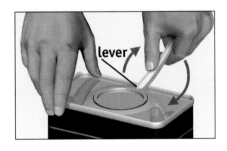

life cycle (līf sī'kəl) The
ordered changes that occur during
the lifetime of a living thing. (A9)
An insect goes through three or
four stages in its *life cycle.*

liquid (lik'wid) A state of matter
that has no definite shape but
takes up a definite amount of
space. (C20) At room temperature,
water is a *liquid.*

lunar eclipse (lōō'nər i klips')
The darkening of the Moon when
it moves into Earth's shadow.
(B76) During a *lunar eclipse,*
Earth blocks the Sun's light from
reaching the Moon directly.

machine (mə shēn') Something that makes a task easy to do by reducing the amount of force needed to do a job. (C72) A *machine* can make it easier to move, lift, carry, or cut something.

magma (mag'mə) Liquid rock deep inside Earth. (D50) After *magma* flows out of a volcano the magma is called lava.

mass (mas) The amount of matter that something contains. (C10) An elephant has more *mass* than an insect.

matter (mat'ər) Anything that has mass and takes up space. (C10) Every living and nonliving thing around you is made of *matter*.

melt (melt) To change form from a solid to a liquid. (C54) Ice *melts* at 0°C (32°F) and iron melts at 1,530°C (2,786°F).

meteorite (mēt'ē ər īt) A chunk of rock or metal that has fallen from space. (B11) A *meteorite* may be as small as a grain of sand or as large as a house.

migrate (mī'grāt) To move to another region as the seasons change. (E74) Many northern birds and butterflies *migrate* south during the winter.

minerals (min'ər əlz) Solids found in nature that have a definite chemical makeup. (D10) Calcium is a *mineral* found in milk and cheese.

natural resource (nach'ər əl rē'sôrs) A material found in or on Earth that people use. (D9) *Natural resources* include water, minerals, fossil fuels, soil, plants, and animals.

nonrenewable resource (nän ri nōō'ə bəl rē'sôrs) A natural resource that cannot be replaced within a person's lifetime. (D11) Diamonds are *nonrenewable resources* because it will take nature millions of years to make more.

nutrient (nōō′trē ənt) Any substance used by living things for energy, growth, repair, or other life processes. (E43) Proteins, carbohydrates, and fats are *nutrients* found in food.

nymph (nimf) The second stage in the life cycle of an insect undergoing incomplete metamorphosis. (A24) A grasshopper *nymph* looks similar to a small adult.

omnivore (äm′ni vôr) An animal that eats both plants and animals. (E18) Because bears will eat both berries and fish, bears are classified as *omnivores*.

opaque (ō pāk′) Materials that block light. (C35) *Opaque* curtains are used in theaters to block the light from windows.

orbit (ôr′bit) The path a planet, moon, or other object takes around another. (B46) The Moon is seen in different phases as it moves through its *orbit* around Earth.

parasite (par′ə sīt) A living thing that, at some point in its life, lives on or in another living thing and harms it. (E52) Fleas, lice, and some kinds of worms are *parasites*.

petal (pet′′l) The brightly colored part of a flower that helps attract birds, bees, and other insects to the flower. (A44) A *petal* is one of the three main parts of a flower.

phase (fāz) Any stage in the series of changes in the apparent shape of the Moon. (B53) The Moon's shape appears to change with each *phase*.

physical change (fiz′i kəl chānj) A change in the size, shape, or state of matter. (C23) When water freezes, it undergoes a *physical change* from a liquid to a solid.

physical property (fiz'i kəl präp' ər tē) A quality of matter that can be measured or observed with the senses without changing the matter into another kind of matter. (C14) A *physical property* of ice is its hardness.

pistil (pis'til) The central part in a flower where seeds form. (A44) For seeds to form in a plant, the pollen must travel to the *pistil*.

planet (plan'it) A large body that orbits a star and does not produce light of its own. (B47) Earth is a *planet*.

pollen (päl'ən) The powdery grains in a flower; they must be carried from a stamen to a pistil in order for seeds to form. (A44) Bees move *pollen* from one flower to another.

pollination (päl ə nā'shən) The process by which pollen reaches a pistil. (A44) After *pollination*, a flower can produce seeds.

pollution (pə loo'shən) Any unwanted or harmful material found in the environment. (D17) Air *pollution* can cause damage to your lungs.

precipitation (prē sip ə tā'shən) The liquid or solid forms of water that fall to Earth. (D31) Rain, sleet, hail, and snow are different kinds of *precipitation*.

predator (pred'ə tər) An animal that hunts other animals for food. (E27) Hawks, cougars, and sharks are *predators*.

prey (prā) An animal hunted for food by another animal. (E27) Rabbits, mice, small fish, and insects are often *prey* for larger animals.

producer (prō doos'ər) A living thing that can make its own food. (E16) Plants, such as trees and grass, are *producers*.

prominence (präm'ə nəns) A huge loop of gas that appears on the edge of the Sun. (B27) *Prominences* are caused by magnetic storms on the Sun.

property (präp'ər tē) Something that describes matter. (C12) A *property* of water in its liquid form is its ability to flow.

pulley (pŏŏl'ē) A wheel around which a rope or chain is passed. (C75) A *pulley* helps lift objects that would be too heavy to lift directly.

pupa (pyŏŏ'pə) The third stage in the life cycle of an insect undergoing complete metamorphosis. (A23) As a *pupa*, an insect is enclosed in a cocoon, or case.

radiation (rā dē ā'shən) The movement of heat energy in the form of waves. (C49) Heat from a campfire reaches you through *radiation*.

renewable resource (ri nŏŏ'ə-bəl rē'sôrs) A natural resource that can be replaced within a person's lifetime. (D11) Lumber is a *renewable resource* if new trees are planted to replace cut trees.

reservoir (rez'ər vwär) The body of water that is stored behind a dam. (D31) A *reservoir* stores fresh water for a town or city.

revolve (ri välv') To move in a circle or orbit. (B46) Earth *revolves* around the Sun.

rotation (rō tā'shən) The spinning motion around an axis. (B38) Earth takes 24 hours to complete one *rotation*.

scale (skāl) A cone's woody part on which seeds grow. (A51) A pine cone's *scales* protect its seeds.

season (sē'zən) Any of the four parts of the year. (B65) The four *seasons* are spring, summer, fall, and winter.

seed coat (sēd kōt) The part of a seed that protects the plant embryo. (A39) The *seed coat* of a coconut is hard, thick, and brown.

seedling (sēd'liŋ) The new plant that develops from an embryo and has roots, a stem, and leaves. (A41) A tomato *seedling* can be started indoors in early spring and planted outside in May.

simple machine (sim′pəl mə shēn′) A device that changes the size or direction of a force. (C73) A lever is a *simple machine*.

soil The loose material that covers much of Earth's surface. (D56) As they grow, most plants extend their roots into *soil*.

solar eclipse (sō′lər i klips′) The blocking of light from the Sun when the Moon moves between it and Earth. (B75) During a *solar eclipse*, the Sun's light is blocked by the Moon.

solar energy (sō′lər en′ər jē) Energy produced by the Sun. (C36) *Solar energy* can be used to produce electricity.

solar system (sō′lər sis′təm) The Sun and all the planets and other objects that orbit it. (B47) Earth is one of nine planets in the *solar system*.

solid (säl′id) A state of matter that has a definite shape and takes up a definite amount of space. (C19, D14) A rock, a piece of ice, and a chair are all examples of *solids*.

species (spē′shēz) A group of living things that can produce living things of the same kind. (A10) The lion *species* cannot produce young of the gorilla *species*.

stamen (stā′mən) The part of a flower that produces pollen, which is needed to form seeds. (A44) *Stamens* are often long and have a fuzzy end.

star (stär) A ball of very hot gases that gives off light and other energy. (B27) The Sun is a *star*.

states of matter (stāts uv mat′r.) The three forms that matter takes—solid, liquid, and gas. (C19) Water exists naturally in all three *states of matter*.

stored energy (stôrd en′ər jē) Energy in matter that can cause matter to move or change. (C31) Fuels have *stored energy* from the Sun.

sunspot (sun′spöt) A dark area on the surface of the Sun, caused by a solar storm. (B27) A *sunspot* appears darker because it is cooler than surrounding areas of the Sun.

surface water (sʉr′fis wôt′ər) Fresh water in lakes, streams, and rivers. (D30) People often pipe *surface water* to nearby cities.

telescope (tel′ə skōp) A device that makes distant objects appear larger and brighter. (B15) A *telescope* is used to study stars and other planets.

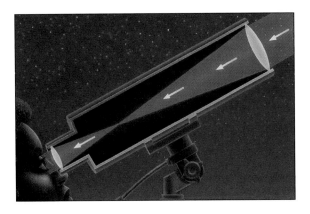

temperature (tem′pər ə chər) A measure of how hot or cold something is. (C45) *Temperature* is measured with a thermometer.

theory (thē′ə rē) A hypothesis that is supported by a lot of evidence and is widely accepted by scientists. (S9) The big-bang *theory* offers an explanation for the origin of the universe.

topsoil (täp′ soil) A mixture of weathered rock and humus (decayed plant and animal matter). (D57) *Topsoil* contains nutrients that help plants to grow.

variable (ver′ē ə bəl) The one difference in the setups of a controlled experiment; provides a comparison for testing a hypothesis. (S7) The *variable* in an experiment with plants was the amount of water given each plant.

volcano (väl kā′nō) An opening in the ground through which hot ash, gases, and lava move from inside Earth to the surface, sometimes forming a cone-shaped hill or mountain. (D51) Lava poured out of the *volcano,* adding a new layer of rock to the land.

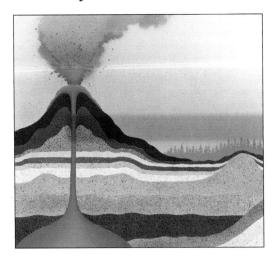

volume (väl yo͞om) The amount of space that matter takes up. (C11) A *volume* of water that measures a pint weighs about a pound.

water cycle (wôt'ər sī'kəl) The path that water follows as it evaporates into the air, condenses into clouds, and returns to Earth as rain, snow, sleet, or hail. (D30) In the *water cycle*, water evaporates from lakes and oceans into the air, and then condenses and falls back to Earth as rain or snow.

water vapor (wôt'ər vā'pər) Water that is in the form of a gas. (D29) Steam, which is invisible, is *water vapor*.

weathering (we*th*'ər iŋ) The breaking up or wearing away of rocks. (D52) Rock formations in Arches National Park have been formed by the *weathering* action of wind and rain.

wetlands (wet'landz) Swamps, marshes, and bogs that are home to many kinds of animals and plants. (E65) *Wetlands* are low-lying areas where water is absorbed into underground aquifers.

wheel and axle (hwēl ənd ak'səl) A simple machine that is made up of two wheels that turn together. (C75) A doorknob, along with its shaft, is an example of a *wheel and axle*.

INDEX

CREDITS

ILLUSTRATORS
Cover: Garry Colby.

Think Like a Scientist: 4–6, 8–9: Garry Colby. 14: Laurie Hamilton. *Borders:* Garry Colby.

Unit A: 8–9: Kathy Rusynyk. 10–11: Steve McInterf. 14–15: A.J. Miller. 22: Doreen Gay Kasssel. 28–29: Adam Mathews. 38: Eldon Doty. 39: *t.* Ka Botzis, *b.* Rebeca Mereles. 44–45: Lori Anzalone. 47, 50, 52: Dan McGowan. 54: Paul Blakey. 58: Julie Carpenter. 61: Lori Anzalone.

Unit B: 7: Richard Courtney. 10: Randy Hamblin. 12–13: Richard Courtney. 14: Stephen Wagner. 20: Jenny Campbell. 21: A.J. Miller. 22: Jenny Campbell. 22: Robert Roper. 23: Jenny Campbell. 27: Richard Courtney. 28: David Barber. 29–31: Richard Courtney. 37: Tom Powers. 39: Verlin Miller. 40: Tom Powers. 42–43: Skip Baker. 44–45: Tom Powers. 46–47: Dennis Davidson. 48–49: Eldon Doty. 51–52, 54: Tim Blough. 55–56: Susan Simon. 57: Tom Powers. 64–65: Liz Conrad. 64–66: Uldis Klavins. 68–69: Jean and Mou-Sien Tseng. 70: Eureka Cartography. 70–71: Traci Harmon. 74–75: Jean and Mou-Sien Tseng. 76: Dennis Davidson. 77: Uldis Klavins.

Unit C: 15, 19–21: Andrew Shiff. 20, 25: Patrick Gnan. 26–27: Susan Simon. 28: Scott Luke. 30–33: Larry Jost. 34–35: Garry Colby. 36: Leslie Wolf. 44–46: Akio Matsuyoshi. 47: A.J. Miller. 49: Robert Roper. 50–51: Randy Hamblin. 54–56: Jim Turgeon. 57: Patrick Gnan. 64–65: Stephen Peringer. 66–67: Eldon Doty. 72: Patrick Gnan. 74: Jeff Stock. 75, 77: Patrick Gnan.

Unit D: 11: Eldon Doty. 14–15: Tim Blough. 16: Mike Kline. 17–18: Tim Blough. 25–27: Bob Brugger. 28: Mike Meaker. 30–31: Stephen Wagner. 31: Dan Clyne. 32–33: Robert Roper. 37: Stephen Bauer. 40–41: Eldon Doty. 42–43: Tom Pansini. 44: Robert Schuster. 45: Tom Pansini. 50: John Youssi. 59: Jeannie Winston. 60: Don Baker.

Unit E: 11–12: Higgins Bond. 16–19: Jim Owens. 20–21: Jeffrey Terreson. 26–27: Jenny Campbell. 27: Jackie Geyer. 28–29: Jenny Campbell. 30: Sarah Jane English. 32–33: Jim Salvati. 35: Jackie Geyer. 44–45: Phil Wilson. 48–53: Jenny Campbell. 54–56: Sarah Jane English. 55: Susan Melrath. 61: Jackie Geyer. 62–63: Deborah Pinkney. 64: Jackie Geyer. 66–67: Eldon Doty. 70–71: Tina Fong. 74–75: Robert Schuster. 77: Deborah Pinkney.

Math and Science Toolbox: *Logos:* Nancy Tobin. 14–15: Andrew Shiff. *Borders:* Garry Colby.

Glossary: 17–18: Richard Courtney. 19: *b.l.* Dan McGowan. *b.r.* Robert Roper. 20: *t.l.* Richard Courtney. *m.r.* A.J. Miller. 21: *m.l.* Liz Conrad. *m.r.* Jeffrey Terreson. 22–23: Stephen Wagoner. 24: Patrick Gnan. 25: Scott Ross. 26: Denise Davidson. 27: Stephen Wagoner. 28: Pat Gnan. 29 Denise Davidson. 30: *t.l.* Stephen Wagoner. *b.r.* Brad Gaber. 31: Stephen Wagoner.

PHOTOGRAPHS
All photographs by Houghton Mifflin Co. (HMCo.) unless otherwise noted.

Front Cover: *t.* Randy Ury/The Stock Market; *m.l.* A & L Sinbaldi/Tony Stone Images; *b.l.* Gary Vestal/Tony Stone Images; *b.r.* Superstock.

Think Like A Scientist: 4–5: Luiz Claudio Marigo/Peter Arnold, Inc.

Table of Contents: xiv: *l.* © James Steinberg/Photo Researchers, Inc.; *m.* © Gary Retherford/Photo Researchers, Inc.; *r.* Zig Leszczynski/Animals Animals/Earth Scenes.

Unit A 1: © Fletcher & Baylis/Photo Researchers, Inc. 2–3: *bkgd* © Fletcher & Baylis/Photo Researchers, Inc.; *inset* © J. Zerschling/Photo Researchers, Inc. 4–5: *bkgd.* Fred Hirschmann; *inset* Erik Hill/Anchorage Daily News. 8: *l.* Dwight R. Kuhn; *r.* Dwight R. Kuhn. 14: E.R. Degginger/Color-Pic, Inc. 16: *t.* E.R. Degginger/Color-Pic, Inc.; *b.* Frans Lanting/Minden Pictures. 17: *l.* Chick Master Incubator Company; *r.* Gil Taylor/Chick Master Incubator Company. 18: *t.* Hans & Judy Beste/Animals Animals/Earth Scenes; *b.r.* © M. Reardon/Photo Researchers, Inc.

19: *t.* Miriam Austerman/Animals Animals/Earth Scenes; *b.l.* Michio Hoshino/Minden Pictures; *b.r.* Frans Lanting/Minden Pictures. 22: *t.l.* Courtesy, Evelyn O'Shea; *t.r.* Courtesy, Evelyn O'Shea; *b.l.* Courtesy, Evelyn O'Shea; *b.r.* Courtesy, Evelyn O'Shea. 23: *t.l.* E.R. Degginger/Animals Animals/Earth Scenes; *t.r.* Patti Murray/Animals Animals/Earth Scenes; *b.l.* Patti Murray/Animals Animals/Earth Scenes; *b.r.* Patti Murray/Animals Animals/Earth Scenes. 25: *t.l.* Raymond A. Mendez/Animals Animals/Earth Scenes; *t.r.* John Pontier/Animals Animals/Earth Scenes; *b.* © David & Hayes Norris/Photo Researchers, Inc. 28: *l.* Anne Heimann; *r.* Anne Heimann. 29: *l.* Anne Heimann; *r.* Trevor Barrett/Animals Animals/Earth Scenes. 30–31: Flip Nicklin/Minden Pictures. 31: Jeff Foott/DRK Photo. 32: *l.* Michio Hoshino/Minden Pictures; *r.* Michio Hoshino/Minden Pictures. 34: © 1994 Jill Krementz. 34–35: *bkgd.* Antonio M. Rosario/The Image Bank. 40: *t.* S. Nielsen/Imagery; *m.* Runk/Schoenberger/Grant Heilman Photography, Inc.; *b.* E.R. Degginger/Color-Pic, Inc. 41: Dwight R. Kuhn. 46: *l.* Superstock; *r.* Superstock. 48: *t.* Grant Huntington for HMCo.; *m.* Grant Huntington for HMCo.; *b.* Grant Huntington for HMCo. 49: *t.r.* E.R. Degginger/Color-Pic, Inc.; *m.* E.R. Degginger/Color-Pic, Inc.; *b.l.* Grant Huntington for HMCo.; *b.r.* E.R. Degginger/Color-Pic, Inc. 53: *t.l.* David Austen/Tony Stone Images; *t.r.* David Austen/Animals Animals/Earth Scenes; *b.* Don Pitcher/Stock Boston. 55: Grant Huntington for HMCo. 56: Grant Huntington for HMCo. 57: *t.* Grant Huntington for HMCo.; *b.* Grant Huntington for HMCo. 58–59: Barry L. Runk/Grant Heilman Photography, Inc. 59: *t.* Runk/Schoenberger/Grant Heilman Photography, Inc. 60: *l.* Runk/Schoenberger/Grant Heilman Photography, Inc.; *r.* Jim Strauser/Grant Heilman Photography, Inc.

Unit B 1: UPI/Corbis Corporation. 2–3: UPI/Corbis Corporation. 4–5: *inset* Victor Aleman/2 Mun-Dos Communications. 11: *l.* NASA; *r.* H.R. Bramaz/Peter Arnold, Inc. 12: NASA/The Stock Market. 13: NASA. 15: *bkgd.* Corbis Corporation; *inset* Frank Rossotto/The Stock Market. 16: *t.* Photri, Inc. 17: NASA. 18: Grant Huntington for HMCo. 19: Grant Huntington for HMCo. 23: *l.* NASA; *r.* © NASA/Science Source/Photo Researchers, Inc. 24: Grant Huntington for HMCo. 25: Grant Huntington for HMCo. 26: Grant Huntington for HMCo. 29: *t.* Photri, Inc.; *b.* © Pekka Parviainen/Science Photo Library/Photo Researchers, Inc. 30: *l.* National Solar Observatory/Sacramento Peak; *r.* NASA/Frank P. Rossotto/Stocktrek. 32–33: E.R. Degginger/Color-Pic, Inc. 34: Grant Huntington for HMCo. 35: *t.* Grant Huntington for HMCo.; *b.* E.R. Degginger/Color-Pic, Inc. 37: *l.* Grant Huntington for HMCo.; *m.* Grant Huntington for HMCo. 38: © Sylvain Grandadam/Photo Researchers, Inc. 40: Dennis Cox/ChinaStock. 40–41: Oddo & Sinibaldi/The Stock Market. 41: *l.* Robert Holmes; *m.* D & J McClurg/Bruce Coleman Incorporated; *r.* Norman Owen Tomalin/Bruce Coleman Incorporated. 52: NASA. 58–59: *bkgd.* John Gerlach/Tom Stack & Associates; *inset* Doranne Jacobson. 62: *t.* Ken Karp for HMCo.; *b.* Ken Karp for HMCo. 63: Ken Karp for HMCo. 67: *bkgd.* Tibor Bognar/The Stock Market; *l. inset* Robert Frerck/Odyssey Productions; *r. inset* D. Donne Bryant. 68: Superstock. 69: *t.* Courtesy, National Maritime Museum. 70: *r.* Superstock. 71: Brian Stablyk/Tony Stone Images. 72: *t.* Ken Karp for HMCo.; *b.* George Post. 73: *t.* Ken Karp for HMCo.; *b.* S.Nielsen/Imagery. 74: Sen Sakamonto/Black Star.

Unit C 1: Adam Woolfitt/Corbis Corporation; 4–5: *bkgd.* G. Bliss/Masterfile Corporation; *inset* Stewart Cohen/Tony Stone Images. 23: *t.* Joyce Design; *b.* Joyce Design. 24: Joyce Design. 29: Grant Huntington for HMCo. 31: PhotoEdit. 32: *t.l.* Grant Huntington for HMCo.; *t.r.* Grant Huntington for HMCo. 33: *t.* Grant Huntington for HMCo.; *m.* Grant Huntington for HMCo.; *b.* Grant Huntington for HMCo. 35: *l.* Uniphoto Picture Agency; *r.* G.K. & Vikki Hart/The Image Bank. 37: David Phillips for HMCo. 38: *t.l.* The Image Bank; *t.r.* Bob Krist/Tony Stone Images. 39: *t.l.* Joe Cornish/Tony Stone Images; *t.r.* Phill Degginger/Color-Pic, Inc.; *b.* Superstock. 48: *l.* Richard Hutchings for HMCo.; *r.* Isaac Geib/Grant Heilman Photography, Inc. 50: *t.* Barry L. Runk/Grant Heilman Photography, Inc. 50–51: John Shaw/Tom Stack & Associates. 51: *b.* Climb High. 54: *t.* Richard Hutchings for HMCo. 55: *t.* Arthur D'Arazien/The Image Bank. 56: *t.* David R. Frazier Photography. 58–59: *bkgd.* Paul Trummer/The Image Bank; *inset* Michael Hampshirengs/National Geographic Society Image Collection.

Unit D 1: John M. Roberts/The Stock Market. 2–3: John M. Roberts/The Stock Market. 4–5: *bkgd.* Bruno P. Zehnder/Peter Arnold, Inc.; *inset* Corazon Claudio. 6: Elliott Smith for HMCo. 8: Frank Rossotto/The Stock Market. 9: *t.l.* Boyd Norton Worldwide Stock Photographs; *b.l.* Steve Wilkings/The Stock Market; *r.* E.R. Degginger/Color-Pic, Inc. 10: Larry Lefever/Grant Heilman Photography, Inc. 17: *l.* © John Meehan/Photo Researchers, Inc.; *r.* © Kent & Donna Dennen/Photo Researchers, Inc. 18: © Dingo Agence Vandystadt/Photo Researchers, Inc. 20: Chris Cone for HMCo. 20–21: John David Fleck/The Gamma Liaison Network. 21: © David M. Grossman/Photo Researchers, Inc. 27: *t.l.* Jeff Smith/The Image Bank; *t.r.* © 2000 Jim Richardson/Woodfin Camp & Associates; *b.l.* Lawrence Migdale Photography; *b.r.* Comstock. 36: Ken Karp for HMCo. 37: *t.l.* E.R. Degginger/Color-Pic, Inc.; *t.r.* © London School of Hygiene and Tropical Medicine/Science Photo Library/Photo Researchers, Inc.; *m.* © Moredon Animal Health, Ltd./Science Photo Library/Photo Researchers, Inc.; *b.l.* Brian Parker/Tom Stack & Associates; *b.r.* © Moredon Animal Health, Ltd./Science Photo Library/Photo Researchers, Inc. 46–47: *bkgd.* PhotoDisc, Inc; *inset* Richard Nowitz Photography. 51: *l.* © Francois Gohier/Photo Researchers, Inc.; *r.* David Stoecklein/The Stock Market. 52: © Douglas Faulkner/Photo Researchers, Inc. 53: © 2000 Leo Touchet/Woodfin Camp & Associates. 56: *t.* E.R. Degginger/Color-Pic, Inc.; *b.* © 2000 William Hubbell/Woodfin Camp & Associates. 56–58: *border* © 2000 Mike Yamashita/Woodfin Camp & Associates. 57: *t.l.* © 2000 G. Fokkema/Woodfin Camp & Associates; *t.m.* Tom Stack for HMCo.; *t.r.* E.R. Degginger/Color-Pic, Inc. 59: © 2000 Robert Frerck/Woodfin Camp & Associates. 60: *t.l.* The Stock Market; *t.r.* © 2000 Robert Frerck/Woodfin Camp & Associates; *b.l.* Carlos Humberto/The Stock Market; *b.r.* Dilip Mehta/The Stock Market. 61: © 2000 Robert Frerck/Woodfin Camp & Associates.